Welcome to Secrets of the Wealth Makers

Premier is honored that our president, Wayne Caldwell, CFP, RFC, is considered one of the top wealth managers in the natio̶ ̶ ̶ ̶e' re not surprised. Mr. Caldwell, along with Premie̶r ̶ ̶ ̶ls, Ron Ross, Ph.D., CFP, and John Gloo̶r ̶ ̶ ̶ ̶mier's professional team to unsurp̶ ̶ ̶ ̶vealth management for families and bu ̶ ̶ r 20 years.

In this book, author Michael La ̶ ̶ ̶ ̶s some of Mr. Caldwell's insights, along with those of other top advisors. The knowledge here is a culmination of years of practical experience helping high net worth people with some of life's difficult wealth management issues. *How do I create wealth for retirement? How do I maintain wealth for my children and grandchildren? Is my portfolio managed to reduce taxes? Do I need estate planning? Will my spouse know how to implement our planning and manage our investments when I'm gone?*

This book is not about finding an investment "guru" or how to make a million dollars overnight. Rather, it imparts professional, ethical and academically proven philosophies for creating and maintaining wealth for your family.

It also underscores the importance of establishing a long-term relationship with a trusted financial advisor, such as Premier. We understand the major reasons that people have difficulty attaining financial peace of mind:

➤ It is hard to stay focused on asset allocation and long-term investing due to "noise" created by Wall Street and the media.
➤ You appropriately use your time to fulfill professional and personal obligations. It is an overwhelming task to filter through the mass of information concerning sophisticated wealth management issues.
➤ It is a daunting process to identify, select and establish a long-term relationship with a trusted advisor.

We hope you enjoy Secrets of the Wealth Makers. This copy is our gift to you. We invite you to pass it along to friends and associates.

Premier Financial Group, Inc.
SEC Registered Investment Advisor
Excellence in Wealth Management

Wayne Caldwell, CFP	Ron Ross, Ph.D., CFP	John Gloor
President ■ Advisor	Principal ■ Advisor	Principal ■ Advisor

725 Sixth Street ■ Eureka, CA 95501 ■ 707.443.2741 ■ 800.331.7212
Fax 707.443.9411 ■ pfg@premieradvisor.com

SECRETS OF
THE WEALTH MAKERS

SECRETS OF THE WEALTH MAKERS

Top Money Managers Reveal Their Investing Wisdom

Michael Lane

McGraw-Hill

New York   San Francisco   Washington, D.C.   Auckland   Bogotá
Caracas   Lisbon   London   Madrid   Mexico City   Milan
Montreal   New Delhi   San Juan   Singapore
Sydney   Tokyo   Toronto

Library of Congress Cataloging-in-Publication Data

Lane, Michael F.
  Secrets of the wealth makers; : top money managers reveal their investing wisdom / by
Michael Lane.
    p. cm.
  ISBN 0-07-135574-X
  1. Investments 2. Finance, Personal. 3. Investment advisers. I. Title.

  HG4521.L3184 2000
  332.6—dc21

                                                                    00-035519

McGraw-Hill

*A Division of The **McGraw·Hill** Companies*

1 2 3 4 5 6 7 8 9 0 AGM/AGM 0 9 8 7 6 5 4 3 2 1 0

ISBN 0-07-135574-X

This book was set in Times New Roman by Inkwell Publishing Services.

Printed and bound by Quebecor World/Martinsburg.

This publication is designed to provide accurate and authoritative information in regard
to the subject matter covered. It is sold with the understanding that neither the author
nor the publisher is engaged in rendering legal, accounting, or other professional service. If legal advice or other expert assistance is required, the services of a competent
professional person should be sought.

> —*From a Declaration of Principles jointly adopted by a Committee of the
> American Bar Association and a Committee of Publishers.*

McGraw-Hill books are available at special quantity discounts to use as premiums and
sales promotions, or for use incorporate training programs. For more information,
please write to the Director of Special Sales, McGraw-Hill, Professional Publishing,
Two Penn Plaza, New York, NY 10121-2298. Or contact your local bookstore.

 This book is printed on recycled, acid-free paper containing a minimum of
50% recycled de-inked fiber.

I dedicate this to my wife, Lisa, and my beautiful children, Kendall and Brooks. My relationship with you is my greatest achievement.

I want to thank Harold Evensky, Lynn Hopewell, John Bowen, Jr., Len Reinhart, Jeff Saccacio, Kelley Schubert, Stan Hargrave, Kim Foss-Erickson, Wayne Caldwell, Joe Campisi, Patrick Moran, Thomas Muldowney, Marilyn Bergen, Ray Ferrara, Glenn Kautt, Tom Nohr, Lance Pelky, Floyd Shilanski, Doug Schreiber, Jr., Mark Sumsion, John Meier, and Douglas Baker for sharing their insights.

I especially want to thank Larry Chambers for helping to coach me through this project. You're a great coach and a better friend.

CONTENTS

Preface   *ix*

Introduction   *xi*

PART 1 WEALTH PLANNING

1	Planning for Wealth	*3*
2	Risk and Risk Tolerance	*25*
3	Diversification and Asset Allocation	*33*
4	Investment Noise	*41*
5	Managing Performance Expectation	*46*

PART 2 WEALTH ACCUMULATION

6	Market Timing	*53*
7	Mutual Fund Selection	*57*
8	Separate Account Managers	*64*
9	E-Trading	*79*
10	Company Stock Options	*93*

PART 3 WEALTH WITHOUT TAX

11   Tax-Efficient Investing   *105*

12   Qualified Plans   *117*

13   Annuities   *122*

14   Municipal Bond Funds   *134*

15   Spiders, Diamonds, and other ETFs   *141*

PART 4 WEALTH PROTECTION AND PRESERVATION

16   Asset Protection   *147*

17   Wealth Replacement Trusts   *154*

PART 5 WEALTH TRANSFER

18   Charitable Remainder Trusts   *163*

19   Estate-Planning Techniques   *170*

      Conclusion   *183*

      Appendix A: Wealth Makers Index   *185*

      Appendix B: Variable Life Insurance   *201*

      Appendix C: Annuity Payment Options   *204*

      Index   *213*

PREFACE

TODAY EVERYONE WATCHES THE STOCK MARKET. Ordinary people know what the market is doing in the middle of any given day, whether or not they are invested. Your favorite Internet sites have the Dow Jones and the Standard & Poor's (S&P) running across the bottom of the screen. Information is abundant and readily available.

Still, the problem is time: People have so little of it to spend on researching and learning. How do you know you are making the right investment decisions? What are the experts saying? Is their advice different from what you've been told? Are you making a leap of investment faith?

After reading many of the top books on investing advice, such as *Market Wizards* and *Investment Gurus*, I realized that they didn't tell me how to implement their insights in a comprehensive investment strategy. There was an unmet need for guidance, and so I set out to interview the top financial advisors to complete the picture. If success leaves clues, the cumulative experience of 25 of the top financial advisors in the country should supply a virtual road map that anyone can follow.

I've been in the investment business for over a decade as both a financial consultant and a creator of investment products. During this time I've had the good fortune to meet and become friends with some of the best and brightest financial advisors in the country—real wealth makers. I have asked them to speak candidly to me about investing and what makes their investor clients successful. The book is structured to make it easy to identify whose opinions and secrets you are reading.

Now, for just a small investment of your time, you can gain the benefit of years of knowledge and experience by reading this book. This book is for intelligent investors who want to glean secrets from leaders in the industry who are actually making other people wealthy and are willing to share their personal investing and financial-planning secrets.

Think of this book as a resource you can consult frequently to help build or adjust your investment strategies or adopt new ones. Just one idea could make a difference in the success of your financial future.

Best of luck!

Michael Lane

INTRODUCTION

INTERESTED TO LEARN how the clients of the top financial advisors have amassed millions of dollars of wealth? Can you duplicate the success of their wealth-making secrets? What do the top financial advisors in the country recommend in order to retire comfortably? Are they playing individual stocks? Are they investing in mutual funds? Are they investing overseas? Are they holding stocks for a week or 10 years? Do they use annuities, variable life, or municipal bonds for tax efficiency? How do they help a person transfer accumulated wealth?

Hi, my name is Michael Lane. I'm president of AEGON Financial Services Group, Inc., Advisor Resources, in Louisville, Kentucky. My firm focuses on helping people like you and your professional investment advisors find successful investment solutions. I've accumulated *hundreds* of years of experience in this book to give you the answers and tell you how to achieve investment success. For the next 200 or so pages I will address several topics ranging from E-trading to estate planning, individual investing to separate managed accounts. The primary objective is to provide you with the experts' opinions on these topics to assist you in finding the best strategy and products.

For the last 12 years I have been intrigued by the attention granted to "hot" portfolio managers. If the market is up 10 percent and a mutual fund manager is up 20 percent, he or she is touted in all the financial media. I read publications such as *Money Magazine* and *Smart Money* and wonder how many of the readers of those "sure bet" investment articles actually implement them and then hold the investments long enough to garnish at least half the potential reward. Buying the hot fund or hot stock of the day is only one, typically faulted, way to approach investing. But let's take the emphasis off the fund manager and place it on the source that actually provides consumers with the advice that can *make or break* a person's retirement.

Financial advisors come in many shapes and forms; some focus on niche opportunities, while others are comprehensive. I have met advisors who work on a fee basis, while others strictly earn commissions for the products they sell. It is not my position in this book to decide that one is better than the other. My objective is to take a detailed yet random sampling of a diverse group of advisors and weed through recommendations that appear consistent.

Every investor's situation is different. To minimize confusion, I have eliminated opinions that are on either end of the spectrum—ultraconservative to overly aggressive—since neither is likely to get you where you want to be in a predictable way.

My goal is to educate you—not about what to buy or whom to buy it from—but about the inside strategies and tactics used by the best in the business. The advisors I interviewed represent over 40 *billion* managed dollars and 30,000 clients. These are some of the most frequently quoted financial planners in the media and the most respected people in the industry. The majority have a minimum of 15 years of experience in the financial services business, and some have more than 30 years. Most of them have assets under management well in excess of $100 million.

The advisors who contributed to this book all have one thing in common: *the desire to meet the needs of their clients.* These people are not product salespeople. (About two-thirds of the people in the securities industry still earn a commission by selling a product.) The members of this group are truly interested in making sure their clients retire comfortably. Their recommendations, along with their personal stories, can help set the stage for you to achieve financial wealth and prosperity. As an advisor is introduced in the book, his or her location will be provided. For more specific information about each advisor, the reader can check Appendix A.

Before you begin Chapter 1, I want you to be in the correct state of mind. Everyone would love to be a "fly on the wall" during confidential, in-depth discussions. This is your chance! While reading through these chapters, visualize yourself in a room where the top financial advisors in the country have gathered together as a sort of focus group. As a topic is outlined, these experts will share their insights into it, strategies they employ, even stories about clients who did or did not follow their advice. You have a wonderful opportunity to learn secrets in a couple of weeks that took me over a year to gather.

WEALTH PLANNING

The objective of this section is to provide you with expert opinion on the planning and implementation steps necessary to achieve wealth.

1

PLANNING FOR WEALTH

WEALTH IS SELDOM ACCRUED OVERNIGHT. You cannot, with any degree of probability, become a multimillionaire without proper planning, and more important, a *commitment*. If you're married or living with a significant other, you must both be committed to building wealth. This may seem like common sense, but believe me, it is more than that. Most of my married friends, both male and female, have issues when it comes to saving money. The most prominent is that one is a saver while the other is a spender. Before you read another page, you must first create an agreement with your spouse or significant other that you both will make an effort to build wealth, which means sacrificing a portion of everyday spending. But you shouldn't sacrifice everything, since that probably will lead to resentment and abandonment of the planning and accumulation phase of wealth building.

For most financial planners, the initial step that must be accomplished before investing is to understand the end objective. This step often is overlooked by most pure investment advisors. As you read this book, you will notice that some of the wealth managers have a foundation in planning while others focus more on investment methodology. I thought it might be helpful for you to hear responses to questions from multiple advisors. That way, as you read the book, you will begin to understand how different wealth managers plan and invest to meet their clients' needs. To make it simple to align the opinions with the advisors, I will start by listing the advisor and his or her location. For more information on each advisor, check Appendix A. Let's start with a few advisors' insights into what an investor must grasp before initiating the planning process.

Tom Nohr, a certified financial planner (FP) from Castro Valley, California, says, "Many people believe that they won't need as much income at retirement and that their taxes will be lower. This is unlikely, and planning that way could be disastrous." I agree. My belief has always been that I do not want to work with a financial planner or investment advisor whose goal is to lower my income at retirement. Your goal should be to retire at the same standard of living you currently can afford. In many situations, this means maintaining your current tax bracket. Tom believes that the first step in planning for wealth is to have a rational understanding of the fundamentals of taxation.

Lynn Hopewell from McLean, Virginia, follows the prudent investment procedures that all the *big money* managers use: "First assess your personal and financial circumstances; then formulate an investment policy that reflects those circumstances. Implement the policy by using a portfolio that is well diversified, economical, and, for taxable funds, tax-efficient. Don't make frequent changes, and don't worry about market dips. Keep your eye on the long term." This is a great place to start for most investors.

Harold Evensky from Coral Gables, Florida, states, "Investors are not necessarily rational. Recognition of the insecurities and emotions of the investor is paramount to successful long-term investing." I agree that emotion has to be put aside when one is planning for wealth. Throughout this book you will note that emotion is a major factor to contend with in the wealth-building process.

John Bowen, Jr., from San Jose, California, agrees: "It is important for investors not to get caught up in the *noise* of the day. Investors are surrounded by many messages that often have nothing to do with making intelligent decisions regarding their investment programs. It is very easy to get seduced when the media sensationalize many of these messages in an attempt to stand out from the crowd. Unfortunately, most of this information will do more harm than good. We believe investors need to move from being *noise* investors who are caught up in day-to-day reactions, to becoming *informed* investors who understand how markets work." John makes a good point in stating that listening to investment noise and making emotional decisions go hand in hand.

Marilyn Bergen from Portland, Oregon, offers another viewpoint: "My investment insights do not involve how to pick the right investment at the correct time. It is critical to take the emotional guesswork and reaction out of the investment decision-making process. This can be achieved through a series of nonemotional questions: What is the investor's goal? What is the dollar amount the investor wants to attain? What is the time frame in which the money will be needed?

"It is important to understand the long history of the markets, including both the expected return and the normal volatility ranges of multiple asset categories. We can then help the client answer the question: How much money needs to be saved annually or monthly to achieve the goal? What rate of return is necessary to achieve the goal? Is that rate of return possible or probable? Will the client be able to live with the volatility associated with that rate of return?

"A plan then can be put in place. Appropriate investments should be chosen to match the time frame in which the money will be needed. The investment plan should be well diversified across several asset classes. Then comes the hardest part: Emotions and reactions to volatility have to be put aside in favor of sticking to the well-thought-out plan."

Kelley Schubert from Dallas, Texas, gives us his take on emotional investing: "There are basically two emotions that lie at the root of every investment decision: fear and greed. Time spent managing these two emotions is much more valuable than time spent managing the investment portfolio itself. When a person makes a large mistake with his or her investments, it almost always is the result of a decision made out of excessive fear or greed. If this is where my clients are most likely to do the most damage to themselves, it is also where I want to concentrate most of my energies."

Ray Ferrara from Tampa, Florida, agrees that the most important thing is to keep people from hurting themselves: "The Internet provides a wealth of information, but information does not translate into knowledge. Because of the roaring market of the past 18 years, and especially the last 4, many people feel empowered and have decided that they can now invest on their own. To do anything and do it well, you must have three things: time, inclination, and knowledge. Most do-it-yourselfers lack at least one of the three, if not more. Others may hurt themselves by thinking that 'things are different' this time. Yes, things may be different, but only until they are not."

Wayne Caldwell from Eureka, California, adds, "A lifetime of wealth management is not a do-it-yourself project despite all the suggestions to the contrary. A well-respected writer in the field estimated that maybe 1 in 10 people has the emotional fortitude, let alone the time, to succeed at do-it-yourself wealth management. I would suggest the actual number may be even lower, especially as the amount of dollars people are responsible for rises."

Floyd Shilanski from Anchorage, Alaska, finds that people are afraid to start investing because of "their fear of making a bad decision, which causes the *deer in the headlights* syndrome. They become stalled and tend to rely on their friends or the company they work for, thus losing their financial independence."

Finally, Douglas Baker from Los Alamitos, California, encourages patience: "Investment decisions made with a sense of urgency usually prove to be wrong. Too often, investors decide on what to invest in long before they employ an investment methodology. Decisions should not be made in a hurry. Another bus always comes along in 10 minutes."

As you can see, the majority of our first few expert advisors agree that emotion can be the major enemy to the fundamental planning process. It is very common for people to set their sights too high and quickly grow frustrated if the results are not what they expect. As you read this book, try to separate your desires from your needs. Once you understand the level of wealth you need to achieve to be comfortable for life, stretch your goals to meet your desires, working backward to establish what has to be done today, next week, next year, and so on. These are the basic elements of financial planning.

WHAT DO OUR ADVISORS THINK ABOUT FINANCIAL PLANNING?

Ray Ferrara had these insights: "Financial planning is the cornerstone of financial independence. While success may come on occasion to those who don't plan, it is more from luck than from skill." Ray doesn't want his clients to rely on luck.

Thomas Muldowney of Rockford, Illinois, adds a twist: "Financial planning is given too much hype. Once certain efficiencies have been implemented (e.g., tax-sheltered saving, tax-deferred saving, tax reduction, low costs, certain loopholes, and estate tax planning), all that is required is the simple yet challenging task of actually saving the money.

"Every financial plan should be well founded in common sense. More than anything else, every single client should have an above-average understanding of how his or her investments are expected to behave. Sadly, this can be manipulated into a sales tool, but if it is done properly, the client will have expectations that are both reasonable and reachable." In other words, an investor should have expectations about market ups and downs as well as an understanding of extreme market volatility, all of which are normal. Investments rarely provide overnight success; they require care, discipline, attention to details, and patience—lots of patience.

Lynn Hopewell agrees and adds that nothing gets accomplished well without analysis and forethought: "You need a financial plan to accomplish objectives that require money. There's a common expression: 'People don't plan to fail, they just fail to plan.'" It's true. Financial planning as a profession has come a long way but still has a long way to go.

Marilyn Bergen believes that financial planning is a wonderful tool to help clients clarify their goals and objectives and quantify what needs to be done to achieve them: "Financial planning can establish a road map for clients to follow. Instead of just hoping or assuming that they will have a comfortable retirement, financial planning can give clients some level of assurance that they will achieve their goals.

"Financial planning is a way to coordinate all the financial aspects of a client's life. Retirement planning can be coordinated with estate planning, investment decision making, and tax planning. Insurance purchases can be coordinated with the need to protect family members and plan for college and retirement. The list is endless. No financial decisions are without an impact on other financial-planning aspects of a person's life.

"I see financial planning as being like a giant jigsaw puzzle. You can put the borders together by answering some basic financial-planning questions, but the fun part comes when you're trying to get all the pieces to fit together. The challenging part of financial planning is that the puzzle is never static. As your personal life, the economy, tax and estate laws, and retirement plans change, what may have been the perfect picture five years ago needs to be reevaluated. When financial planning is viewed as an ongoing process, it is extremely beneficial in helping individuals achieve wealth."

Wayne Caldwell, like Tom Muldowney, cautions that "comprehensive financial planning as it is currently defined is the accumulation of data and the production of an elaborate and rather long, formal document usually presented in an attractive binder. It has more appearance than substance." As a CFP, he believes in a financial-planning approach to client relationships and decision making: "All of us have limited capabilities to stay focused on complex personal financial-planning issues. Many of these issues are fraught with emotion, interpersonal family dilemmas, and real-world issues that affect the way we try to implement these plans. The advisor's responsibility is to keep the big picture in view and help the client make those pressing decisions in the context of lifelong financial planning.

"Financial planning works best in the context of a formal comprehensive financial relationship with a trusted advisor. Although computer-based financial plans are useful, it appears that all the attempts by large firms and software developers to reduce them to a mechanical approach have been, for the most part, unsuccessful. Financial planning is much more of a process that goes on throughout a client's life than a process of producing a document. In many ways the document is somewhat outdated upon its completion."

Kim Foss-Erickson from Roseville, California, tells her clients that financial planning is an integral part of wealth accumulation, reservation, and transfer to the next generation: "One must consult a road map and/or guide to reach his or her destination if he or she has never traveled there before. An essential part of wealth management is establishing a financial road map that effectively delivers a succinct plan to get to the client's goal in the most effective manner possible."

Douglas Baker, however, believes that comprehensive financial planning may be a thing of the past. In his experience, clients are more likely to seek simple answers to specific issues, such as retirement, education, and estate problems: "It seems that the industry is splintering into those whose expertise may lie in no more than one of these issues. Brokerage firms that cater to the more unsophisticated investor seem to be the only ones promoting comprehensive plans, which are really nothing more than boilerplate sales devices."

So who is right? I would cast my vote somewhere in the middle. I agree with Doug that some financial services firms sell investors a plan merely to sell them financial products. With this said, the majority of the planners I have met, and I have met over 5000, use the plan as a road map, and as a selling tool. Just as in building a home, without a detailed blueprint, one does not know where to start and what the finished product is meant to look like.

SUCCESS STORIES

I asked the members of the group to share success stories about how they achieved wealth for their clients as a result of comprehensive financial planning.

Lynn Hopewell told us that he considers it a success every time he talks a client out of a bad decision and into a good one. He remembers taking a client away from a high-risk strategy and onto a more prudent path. He believes he raised the probability of clients accomplishing their goals by lowering their investment return expectations: "Sometimes they are doing something quite egregious, and we fix that. The key is getting as many things right as possible."

When Glenn Kautt from McLean, Virginia, was asked to supply a planning success story, he described a couple who had repeatedly attempted to create wealth by investing in home run potential investments. Unfortunately, most of these types of investments strike out. They promise big returns but don't deliver in the end. Glenn developed an investment strategy for this couple that allowed for a limited number of higher-risk investments to satisfy their need for thrills while investing the majority of their assets in a portfolio diversified to reduce volatility while reaching the target rate for returns. The financial plan helped the couple realize they could become financially independent without taking undue risk. They finally understood that a consistently applied investment strategy is the quickest route to accumulating wealth.

John Bowen, Jr., told us about one of his first clients, who was very interested in leaving money to his alma mater. John said the gentleman wouldn't have shared that with him if he had not first gone through the process of creating a comprehensive financial plan. Once John understood the client's goals and how they could work in conjunction with his relatively high income, it was very easy to establish a series of charitable trusts and wealth replacement trusts in the form of irrevocable insurance trusts. That plan maximized the current income tax benefits and provided substantial income benefits both to the client in the use of charitable remainder trusts and to the charity through charitable lead trusts. After his client passed away, the client's family realized the benefit of using an estate tax basis of the wealth replacement trust.

A few years ago Wayne Caldwell had a client who needed to implement a retirement plan for the family business to improve employee retention and overall competitiveness. Wayne was successful in implementing a profit-sharing plan and an employee-funded 401(k) plan. During this process the client's father passed away, leaving the client responsible for the firm, although the client's mother was the majority owner of the company. There were also a brother and sister who were not actively involved in the company's operations. Additionally, the mother later married a man who was also one of Wayne's clients. Through all these connections, Wayne became familiar with the entire family's overall financial picture and many of its personal issues.

After some time the mother passed away. All of her estate planning began to be utilized for the transfer of the business and her personal wealth to the three children. Wayne's role expanded dramatically. His initial client sought to acquire the other brother and sister's ownership interest in the business. Wayne assisted in evaluating the value of the company and acquiring a large term life insurance policy to facilitate a buy-sell agreement. This, combined with the impact of the inheritance, became a two-year process of wealth transfer. Wayne worked with the heirs to complete estate planning for each one and establish investment portfolio strategies to receive the inherited funds.

This type of intergenerational management of wealth goes far beyond the confines of traditional financial planning. It creates the need for high-net-worth individuals to establish a comprehensive financial relationship with a competent, experienced financial advisor. Wayne didn't believe it would have been practical or even possible to summarize all those steps and issues in a written document before the fact. It was a process that developed and unfolded over a period of years.

Kim Foss-Erickson recalled that early in her career as a financial planner a young couple in their late twenties approached her to help them devise a financial plan. This included all six areas of the financial-planning process: cash flow/budgeting, education, retirement, taxation, life, and estate planning. They also established an insurance policy on the husband for $500,000 and one for $250,000 on the wife, since both spouses worked and had two small children. Tragically, seven years later, the wife was diagnosed with cancer and died within two years.

The husband was devastated. He had two small children to care for and a job that took him away from home for weeks at a time. The proceeds from a life insurance policy acquired through the couple's planning process enabled him to hire a nanny until he was able to bring his career closer to home. The client and his children were able to deal with the tragedy without financial distress, and today they are all living a very happy and fulfilling life. To Kim, that equates to a real success that makes her role as a planner worth the extra effort.

While listening to the success stories that were shared by all the advisors, I noticed a common thread. Nearly every story outlined the devastation that might have affected multiple generations if proper planning and discipline had not been achieved. While people usually create a financial plan with the immediate family in mind, they often forget about the far-reaching effects.

THE BIG FIVE

We have heard the success stories of those who have planned properly, but what do our experts believe are the five most important things a person needs to know when beginning the planning process?

Harold Evensky:

1. Realistic expectations and controlled emotions
2. Patience
3. Basic investment knowledge of how markets operate
4. Basic knowledge of how investment products work
5. Understanding of the role of risk

Lynn Hopewell and Glenn Kautt collaborated on their answer to this question.

They have dedicated the resources of the firm to helping their clients understand five keys to long-term success:

1. Developing a set of realistic financial goals
2. Assessing the future probabilities of those goals to determine the appropriate level of risk and return required to assure a specific probability of success
3. Managing the outcome of the financial goals by using a consistently applied investment strategy
4. Regularly assessing investment risk and return
5. Reviewing financial goals regularly, modifying them as circumstances dictate, and modifying the associated investment strategy as noted in steps 2 through 4

John Bowen, Jr:

1. Understand the difference between good diversification and bad diversification. Many investors invest in only one security or one asset class, such as U.S. large. This subjects them to significant risk that in the long term doesn't make sense.
2. Think globally. Opportunities exist all over the world today. However, don't invest overseas to obtain higher rates of return; instead, invest to obtain broader diversification, which lowers risk. The expected rates of return of similar-risk companies are the same, whether the companies are domestic or international.
3. Understand dissimilar price movements. Investors often believe they are going to lower their rates of return by holding asset classes that don't perform well along with the top-performing asset class. This would be true if one could predict which asset class was going to outperform the others. Since that is not the case, we create a dissimilar price movement by having asset classes that don't tend to move together, lowering the volatility of the overall portfolio.

4.   Understand that markets are efficient. Individual investors cannot extract value from the market. The cost of trying to do so is extremely high, and chasing gurus who say they can do it costs even more. The bad news is that gurus don't exist; the good news is that you don't need them. If all an investor does is try to capture the market return, on average he or she will outperform 75 percent of all investors.

5.   The most important thing is to understand your personal limitations. Most investors are better off working with a professional financial advisor who can help them organize and put together a written plan covering where they are now and where they want to go and guiding them along the way to make sure they reach their goals.

John likens the concept of diversification to buying life or home-owner's insurance at the beginning of the year. At the end of the year you're looking at the fact that your house didn't burn down and you're still alive, but you're disappointed because you wasted the premium money. Investors need to recognize that the diversification risk premium is worthwhile and allows them to have greater wealth over the long term.

Ray Ferrara:

1.   Know that you need a plan, develop one, and then follow it.

2.   Know your tolerance for risk and find investments that you understand within those limits.

3.   Know that unless you have the time, inclination, and knowledge, you need the help of a certified financial planner.

4.   Know that you need to make economic decisions, not tax-motivated ones, when it comes to your investments.

5.   Know what you don't know. As with most things, those who know the most and put forth the most effort generally do the best.

Marilyn Bergen:

1.   Understand the historical probabilities of expected rate of return and risk volatility.

2.   Understand the importance of diversification.

3.   Develop an investment plan to match your time horizon before the money is needed and match your willingness to live with the volatility associated with the chosen investment plan.

4.   Factor the tax implications and inflation into investment decisions in choosing specific investments.

5.   Be patient and stay the course. Rebalance back to your chosen plan.
      Don't allow emotional guesswork to influence investment decisions.

Kelley Schubert:

1.   Stay disciplined. Do not allow short-term fluctuations in the market
      to cause you to change your long-term investment plan.
2.   Beware of your emotions and learn how they influence your invest-
      ment decisions.
3.   Diversification is always your friend.
4.   What you take home after you pay your taxes is the most important
      thing.
5.   Two heads are better than one. All individual investors will be better
      off if they have a person to whom they are accountable for their
      investment decisions. This can be an advisor or a friend, so long as
      it's someone you trust.

Wayne Caldwell:

1.   You must manage your human relationship with the investment mar-
      ketplace. Personal and family financial issues can be charged with
      emotions. You must understand that while you may not be able to
      change your feelings or emotions, you can manage your investment
      behavior.
2.   You must come to an understanding about the role of the investment
      media. The real awakening comes for each individual investor when
      he or she understands that not only will this financial information
      not be particularly useful in creating successful investment strate-
      gies, the roar of the media is probably the greatest problem in main-
      taining emotional financial stability and a long-term focus.
3.   Nothing will be more valuable or increase your chance of success
      more than a relationship with a trusted financial advisor.
4.   Your investment strategy must be incorporated into a concept of
      long-term investing structured and monitored over a lifetime and,
      for many high-net-worth clients, directed toward the benefit of the
      next generation. Incorporating this view of the world will add
      tremendously to the quality of the relationship with your advisor,
      tone down the roar of the media, and help keep you from losing
      sleep.
5.   You must develop an understanding of your risk tolerance and how
      it will be incorporated into your investment portfolio. This will give
      you the ability to balance risk and return more effectively in the
      portfolio, increasing return and financial peace of mind.

Joe Campisi, from Norristown, Pennsylvania:

1. It's time in the market, not timing.
2. Diversify across asset classes.
3. Buy low, and if you must sell, sell high.
4. Don't focus on the short term with long-term vehicles (stocks, equity funds).
5. Don't let emotions take over. Establish expectations.

Patrick Moran, from Phoenix, Arizona:

1. Have patience.
2. Invest for the long term.
3. Invest in quality.
4. Know why you're investing.
5. Pay yourself monthly.

Douglas Baker:

1. You don't have any more insight into the markets than does the guy down the street.
2. Time is your friend; urgency is not.
3. Emotions make many a cold night wonderful but add nothing to investment decisions.
4. Never buy what you do not understand.
5. Money has only one purpose: to make you sleep well at night. If financial decisions keep you awake, your strategy has failed.

WHAT PROCESS DO YOU USE WHEN PLANNING SOMEONE'S FUTURE?

John Bowen, Jr., believes in a financial-planning checkup that focuses on a reality check in which he looks at the client's current assets and what the client can earn from them. Then he looks at the client's liabilities, including not only debts but also cash-flow needs (retirement, second home, children's education).

Next he runs a "Monte Carlo" simulation to determine the probability of funding the client's goals. Very few investments have a 100 percent probability; most have a probability of 50 percent or less. When the client understands this probability, it's much easier to help the client make smart decisions about his or her money.

Lynn Hopewell describes financial planners as architects who are helping someone plan a new home. The most important factor in building a new home is to understand who is going to live there. A home designed for a family with five young children is different from a home designed for empty nesters. No matter how well constructed it is or how competent the subcontractors are, a house that doesn't fit the needs of the occupants is a failure. After getting the design right, the architect has to do a good job of finding subcontractors and monitoring their work. He or she sometimes has to alter the design of the house to take into account new circumstances.

Ray Ferrara shared his personal 10-step program. (I included this list because it is important to understand what you should expect from an advisor. Ray has outlined what I believe to be the textbook relationship from the beginning.)

1. The first step is to have a "discovery meeting" with a laundry list of the things the client should bring. At the meeting, the prospective client answers questions for about 60 to 90 minutes about finances, family, attitudes, fears, strengths, goals, experiences, health, special needs, and so on. The client completes a very thorough risk tolerance evaluation questionnaire.

2. Several professionals at Ray's firm then meet to review the notes and information. This team puts together the initial ideas to formulate the plan.

3. The next step is to prepare a rough draft of the plan. This takes several weeks. There are typically a dozen or more phone calls with the client to clarify issues and answer new questions. The professional team then meets again to review the preliminary plan.

4. When the plan is completed, a senior member (a CFP) of the financial planning department reviews it. Suggestions and revisions are made.

5. At the plan presentation Ray sets the stage by letting the client know that this meeting is going to be a "show-and-tell" session. No decisions are expected to be made. Ray provides an overview of the plan and answers any questions. He asks the client to take the plan home and read it carefully in the next 48 hours. The client should underline, write questions in the margin, and so on. There are three possible courses of action the client can then take:

- The client can reject the plan.
- The client can accept the plan and implement it personally or have the financial planner or broker implement it.
- The client can accept the plan and have Ray implement it.

6. Ray arranges a meeting within a week to 10 days of the plan presentation to answer all the client's questions. If the client decides to implement the plan, the necessary paperwork and documents are prepared.

7. A meeting is arranged with any other professionals who need to be involved in the plan's implementation (attorney, accountant, and so on).

8. Once the information is gathered, an investment policy statement is written that clearly outlines what Ray is obligated to do as well as what he is prohibited from doing in regard to the client's investment portfolio. The client is given the choice of working on a fee or a commission basis.

9. They begin to implement the plan.

10. Ray monitors the plan and provides detailed quarterly reports. Regular contact is made with the client by phone and in person.

The relationship with each client evolves differently, but a standardized procedure like the one outlined above provides a consistent experience for each client.

Kelley Schubert has a strategy for planning someone's future and identifying how to fill any financial gaps that exist: "The most important thing is to maintain balance. I often joke with my clients that if they die too young, they will mess up their whole financial plan. Although it's just a joke, it has very real implications for a correct financial plan. None of us know how long we will be here, and so my goal as a planner is to put together a plan that achieves both short-term gratification and long-term retirement security. Because these two goals are almost always conflicting (except when my client gets short-term gratification from hoarding money), part of my job is to make sure that the client sacrifices the correct things in both the short term and the long term."

Kelley usually is able to fill the gaps that exist in the financial plan by prioritizing the client's expenses and then seeing how much money is being spent on the lower-priority items. He told us to try this ourselves: "You will be astonished at how much money we spend on low-priority items." The reality is that many people sacrifice long-term retirement freedom and security for things that are very low priority items in the short term. Identifying this disparity is the job of a good financial planner.

Marilyn Bergen helps her clients by clarifying their financial-planning goals by taking the following steps:

- Take a snapshot of where the client currently stands. A balance sheet is a good tool. A cash-flow analysis is useful if the clients need to save more money.
- Assess what the clients have done to date.
- Ask many questions about what's important to them, what they value, what they'd like to accomplish, and what gives them peace of mind.
- Help them develop and clarify financial-planning goals.
- Run scenarios to look at their desired financial situation and alternative situations.
- Quantify and outline what they need to do to achieve their desired or alternative goals.
- Make an action item list of things they need to do to implement the decision.
- Periodically review the situation, depending on the amount of time before the goal is to be achieved.

Wayne Caldwell sees a major dilemma in financial planning today. "Many practitioners, usually young or inexperienced, rely too heavily on computerized plans. The true art of financial planning is to have knowledge, experience, and expertise come together to interpret and implement these plans. There are no perfect answers and there is no set of assumptions that is absolute."

He feels that advisors need to help clients understand what they need to do versus what they would like to do: "Defining the money needs for a college education or a successful retirement is a fairly straightforward mathematical process. People with limited wealth need to make a trade-off between how much will go to support the current lifestyle versus paying for a college education and/or retirement.

"Higher-net-worth people have a substantially different reality and don't usually have such clearly defined goals. Their wealth accumulation is sufficient to send their children and grandchildren through college if they choose. Their potential retirement income, combined with the pool of wealth they've accumulated, will already generate more income than they will need. Their focus is much more on wealth management, tax management, and sophisticated levels of estate planning, charitable planning, and gifting strategies to maximize the transfer of wealth to the next generation.

"Our duty is to help clients deal with the well-known changes that may affect people as they go through life, such as marriage, children, retirement, and death. Financial plans need to be made; however, they must be flexible and subject to review on an ongoing basis. They also must be viewed as guideposts rather than as a straight road from here to there."

To truly understand the pros and cons of planning, one has to understand the obstacles that must be overcome to achieve wealth. We have heard a little about the part emotion plays, but which other obstacle may be encountered?

WHAT OBSTACLES HAVE YOU ENCOUNTERED WITH YOUR INVESTORS?

Harold Evensky explained that the biggest obstacles are inexperience, inertia, unrealistic expectations, and humanness. Investors who cannot detach themselves emotionally from their investments are going to experience a lot of stress.

Lynn Hopewell's biggest obstacle is clients' ideas that journalists know something about investing, that one can predict the market, that success requires making a big killing, and that investing is easy.

Glenn Kautt has developed an investment policy that helps overcome one of the biggest obstacles for his investors: matching investment expectations with the practical realities of one's financial situation: "Investors are rarely able to assess the level of risk associated with their personal investing. Along the same line, they cannot determine the risk/return combination in the overall portfolio that gives them a high probability of achieving their financial goals."

Kelley Schubert agrees with Harold Evensky that the biggest obstacle is the human element. "The human element is born from emotions (fear and greed), pride, self-esteem, peer pressure, and other similar elements that have very little to do with objective investing but tend to be the dominant decision-making factors for the average investor. The human element in us causes people to:

1. Chase the action: Buy or sell stocks immediately after large movements.

2. Trade too often: Engage in unnecessary activity that makes people think they are making progress.

3. Hold on to losers too long: People do not want to admit that they made a poor decision, and so they resist selling.

4. Buy popularity: People don't want to be left out, and so they buy what everyone else is buying.

5. Be overconfident: Everyone thinks the information or the research he or she has is the most accurate. If the market says otherwise (by the way it has priced a stock), people like to think that they are smarter than the market."

Kelley believes that his job as an investment advisor is to "help clients recognize and understand when they are allowing their human nature to affect their investment decisions to their own detriment."

Wayne Caldwell says that the biggest obstacles are a lack of general understanding regarding risk and return and not knowing how to incorporate that understanding into realistic long-term expectations: "Many investors take too much risk for the potential return or invest too conservatively. They have unrealistic expectations and get overwhelmed by marketing and media hype."

"Another obstacle," Wayne adds, "is investors' attraction to the *black box* investment strategy or the guru. This chasing of performance and the corresponding desire to beat the market in order to be a winner, although much promoted in the financial services industry, are not a model that is likely to be successful over the long run. Luck may be with you from time to time, but decade after decade of successful investment experience requires adherence to a realistic investment strategy based on proven portfolio concepts, combined with trust and confidence in your advisor to give you the emotional fortitude to stay the course."

Lance Pelky from San Diego, California, made the point that the biggest fee you will ever pay is to the IRS: "Overcoming that obstacle through proper tax planning is critical."

Finally, Tom Nohr cited one of the biggest obstacles of all: procrastination.

WHEN THINGS GO WRONG

Before continuing on to Chapter 2, how about a reality check. Let's ask our advisors to tell us about times when things didn't work out.

Lynn Hopewell had several of these instances but stated that the common denominator is that a client falls in love with a particular investment that represents most of the client's net worth. These clients reject his advice to diversify because of an irrational belief that the investment "has been good to them." In so many words, Lynn informs these clients that the investment doesn't *know* them and doesn't *care* about them. He tries to get them to understand that they are dangerously exposed when they have most of their eggs in one basket. In each of these cases, when the investment inevitably falls significantly in value, the client bails out at a low point.

Ray Ferrara received a call from a prospective client who had sold his business interest for approximately $3 million. It was more than enough money to support the client's lifestyle for the rest of his life. He was in his early fifties. Ray suggested a written plan and a conservative investment program that would provide income with growth. Instead, the prospect chose to go to a stockbroker who started him in mutual funds and eventually got him into trading Internet stocks and options on margin. In the meltdown of August 1998, he lost it all.

Marilyn Bergen has a sad story that occurred during late summer 1998 with a new client. She had implemented an investment portfolio over 9 to 10 months, using dollar cost averaging into equities. The large cap U.S. market lost approximately 20 percent, and other equity categories also had significant losses. At about the same time she sent a position paper to the client with some thoughts about Y2K issues and potential investment implications. This client responded by wanting to sell his equity positions immediately. She tried to encourage him to consider spreading the sales over several months, a method-reverse-dollar cost averaging, but the client insisted on liquidating all the positions at once. Within two months the stock market started to rebound.

Wayne Caldwell believes that the lack of a good fit between a professional investment advisor and a client does not become apparent until later in the relationship. He told us about a couple in their late sixties who came to see him for help with their financial and estate-planning needs. The clients had received financial advice in a haphazard way over the years and had assets with one or two different stockbrokers and some with a bank. The bulk of their net worth was in real estate, both captive inside an outdated corporation and on a personal level. Their real estate holdings represented a variety of commercial and multi- and single-family dwellings.

These clients seemed overwhelmed by all the decisions and complexities involved in functioning as landlords. This was negatively affecting their senior years and, more important, their relationship with their children. As Wayne organized and simplified their investment assets into a cohesive portfolio and dealt with the ultimate estate tax issues, the clients began to resist his recommendations.

Over the five or six years during which Wayne worked with these clients, the results were mediocre at best. Although Wayne had organized the assets and simplified the clients' lives dramatically, his plans to manage taxes and increase liquidity for the client were not implemented. The client and his wife were still overwhelmed by the daily routine needed to maintain their properties and the multitude of decisions at a time when they really needed to relax, travel more, and enjoy their lives.

This story came to an end when Wayne received a request for a transfer to a stockbroker at a major brokerage firm. Unfortunately, in the process of transfer and without counsel, the clients sold all their long-term assets and created excessive capital gains.

Kelley Schubert got a call in September 1998, just after a 10 percent drop in the market, saying that the client wanted to sell one-half of the stock funds in his portfolio because "things just didn't look good for the future." Kelley told the client that the drop was a short-term fluctuation and that he was strongly against making a long-term investment decision based on it. Against Kelley's advice, the client sold. During the upcoming three months, the S&P 500 regained the 10 percent it had lost in the third quarter and added another 11 percent of profit, for a total fourth quarter gain of 21 percent.

That turned out to be one of the strongest quarters in the history of the S&P 500. Unfortunately, Kelley's client came out a loser for the year because he allowed fear to influence him into selling at exactly the wrong time. More important, he allowed fear of short-term events to cause him to make a decision that did not fit his long-term investment plan.

This type of thinking is always a mistake, even when the perceptions of the future turn out to be correct. Success is achieved by staying true to one's long-term investment plan.

The downside seems to occur when clients chase past returns. Most of the stories that advisors tell center on client's becoming disenchanted with their investment returns and trying to take control themselves. This often leads to mistakes such as selling and creating gains, chasing last year's hot returns, and believing that one can trade on-line and hit the next hot initial public offering (IPO). What appears evident is that clients in most situations would do better to consult with their advisor, establish the fact that their investment objectives are consistent with the portfolio created by the advisor, and then make minor modifications. The objective is to keep taxes to a minimum and maximize long-term investment returns. Don't let one year's disappointment create a multiyear headache.

CHAPTER 2

RISK AND RISK TOLERANCE

I HEAR PEOPLE TALK ABOUT risk as if it were something a person could trip over in the road, but risk is really the investor's friend. Without it, you would be standing in a bank line waiting for the certificate of deposit (CD) window to open. No risk, no reward, as they say. I asked one of our advisors to describe the approach to risk he takes with his clients.

Don Schreiber, Jr., CFP and president and chief executive officer (CEO) of Wealth Builders, Inc., in Little Silver, New Jersey, has spent the last 20 years working with affluent clients who come to his firm for investment advice and management when they are nearing or are in retirement. Over the years he has identified certain common traits in investors who fit into this category.

Almost without exception, these clients sit at the conference table and tell Don that this is all the money they have to live on, so "don't lose it!" They tell him they don't have the time or desire to try to put together another nest egg. This has led him to develop an investment management process for the money clients cannot afford to lose. (Even younger, more aggressive investors acquire a healthy concern for their capital once they are involved in the investment process.)

Don has found that investors' attitudes toward risk in investing their money need to be investigated thoroughly before one makes investment decisions. Much has been written about evaluating investment risk tolerance, but the most critical factor—*investor risk*—is often overlooked.

In the process of building an investment strategy, time and attention typically are spent identifying, assessing, and addressing various investment risks. Just as dangerous to the ultimate success of an investment program, however, is the risk emotions can place on investors' behavior. In Don's opinion, any investment policy that does not address this risk is deficient. Don has prepared the following explanation and test as a way to measure investor risk.

INVESTOR RISK

Much investment theory is based on the premise of the rational investor. Experience suggests, however, that people are heavily influenced by their emotional responses to financial issues in making investment decisions. To win the investment game, clients must stick with their investment programs. If they have failed to measure their inherent investor risk accurately, they will abandon the plan in a market decline and do irreparable financial harm to themselves. This natural tendency can lead investors into critical errors, including the following:

- *Making inappropriate responses to perceived risk.* Greed and fear are opposite sides of the same coin. "Buy low and sell high" is easy to understand. Still, falling prices often cause investors to avoid investments with exceptional values, and soaring prices can create manias as investors ignore real risks—*and their own risk profiles*—to chase today's hottest idea.

- *Attaching too much importance to initial experience.* First impressions are *lasting* impressions. An investor's early experience with a new portfolio strategy can color his or her feelings about everything that follows. A good initial experience can lead to unrealistic expectations and disappointment with what are actually excellent long-term performance results. A bad initial experience can lead to a premature judgment that a strategy is failing even if it is supported by sound investment principles with a long history of superior results and have a high probability of future success. In fact, initial results have far less to do with the merits of an investment strategy than they do with the purely circumstantial accident of whatever market events happened to coincide with the start of the investment program.

- *Adopting too narrow a perspective on the investment universe.* References to "the market," the S&P 500, or the Dow Jones Industrial Average are common in conversations about investments. Daily news accounts of the movements of those entities can keep them in the forefront of investors' attention. However, there's much more to the universe of investable assets than the slice represented by the large company U.S. domestic stocks these indexes measure.

- *Focusing too much attention on the wrong things.* The emotional noise swirling around financial news can cause investors to lose sight of the real purpose of their investment efforts. Relative success against artificial market "benchmarks," irrespective of the risks to an investor's goals, is not the point. Giving oneself the best opportunity to consistently earn *the return one needs* to achieve one's goals— *with the least risk to one's ultimate success*—is the point.

The table that follows shows the stark contrast from an emotional standpoint between the perfect investment and the reality of being an investor.

There's no such thing as a perfect investment. An exceptional investment plan, however, will include strategies to sustain the emotional comfort one needs to avoid the pitfalls of investor risk.

Another aspect of risk is what Don calls the *loss principal.*

THE PERFECT INVESTMENT
VERSUS
THE REALITY OF INVESTING

The Perfect Investment	*The Reality of Investing*

High absolute returns regadless of the ups and downs of the economy or any particular market.	Returns are tied to a complex system of interactive markets and world economies.

High relative terms, outperforming everything else.	No matter what a person has invested in, something, somewhere will be doing better.

No risk of loss. No down days—**ever**.	There are many kinds of risk, and every investment will suffer a loss at some point from at least one of them.

A **guaranteed outcome** at least as good as one needs to reach one's goals.	Guaranteed future outcomes are an illusion. Events in the future can only be more or less likely to occur.

Simplicity—easy to understand and easy to track so that an investor can watch his or her progress toward the goal every day.	Investments involve many complex ideas. Summaries, benchmarks, standards, and disclaimers are simply attempts to provide a context for understanding where an investor is in a fluid system that probably has already changed.

Peace of mind, confidence, and pride in being wise enough to possess such an exceptional asset.	Investments can arouse all kinds of feelings, including fear, envy, remorse, uncertainty, confusion, and greed.

LOSS PRINCIPAL

Before investing, you need to ask yourself how much of your investable assets you are willing to lose if market volatility goes against you. For example, let's say you have just invested $500,000 in a diversified portfolio of equities, get your first account statement a month later, and still have $500,000. You may be somewhat disappointed that the account has not yet grown, but you are comforted that you still have what you started with.

The next month, you open your statement and the account value is $475,000. You call your investment advisor, and he explains that you are experiencing some short-term volatility and that the account is down only 5 percent. You tell the adviser that your account is down $25,000 of your hard-earned money, money that you can't afford to lose.

The following month, your statement indicates that your account value has fallen to $400,000, and you have an identical conversation with the advisor. He says the account is down only 20 percent, well within the normal fluctuations one should expect as an investor. However, you are thinking to yourself, It is not his $100,000. Will you go ballistic or stay the course?

To be a successful investor, you must be willing to stay invested in the long term. Before you invest, you should know your *risk tolerance*—how much you are willing to see your account value decline—and make investment decisions accordingly. This will keep you from selling at the wrong time and losing principal you can't afford to lose.

RISK TOLERANCE

Risk tolerance is really a feeling. It's been described as the point in a decline when investor's feel so much emotional pressure that they are compelled to liquidate their positions in order to relieve their anxiety. If you are willing to ride the investment roller coaster through periods of double-digit advancement and declines, you are probably very risk tolerant. I know people who stay up nights worrying over the possibility of losing even 2 percent of their investment, and so they cash in, run to the bank, and buy CDs. They have a low risk tolerance. There's nothing wrong with that; just don't expect to make stock market returns.

How large of a one-year decline in the value of your portfolio would you be likely to accept before changing your investment strategy?

Percentage Decline	Change in Account Value
5	From $100,000 to $95,000
8	From $100,000 to $92,000
12	From $100,000 to $88,000
20	From $100,000 to $80,000
30	From $100,000 to $70,000

Earlier in my career I was given some shorthand tips that were supposed to help investors make decisions about the amount of risk that they should assume, but found that the majority of those tips were based on age-related criteria. The most basic formula is to subtract the person's age from 100, and the remainder is the percentage that should be invested in more aggressive investment vehicles. However, these tips have little application in the real world of financial planning.

For instance, assume that your home was traded like a stock and its value was measured every day, hour, or even minute. Every blip in interest rates, every local company's relocation, and even a late trash pickup could cause a rise or drop in the value of a home. Major universities would produce studies on the valuation of homes, and experts would surface. Some of those experts would argue that the real estate market could be timed for maximum value; academics would produce evidence to the contrary. Sound familiar?

Soon real estate brokers would not be able to leave their offices to show homes, fearing price changes while they were gone. Real estate magazines would publish performance records of real estate brokers. Investors would keep their suitcases packed, ready to chase the next hot housing development. Every day you would wonder whether you should sell your house or hold it, forgetting that you live there, your children will grow up there, and so on. Rationality would take a back seat to investment noise.

As with the stock market, short-term price changes (volatility) would affect only short-term speculators. The guy who owns his home and has no thoughts of selling it wouldn't bother checking newspapers for the latest price quotes; the guys out for a quick buck would.

The point is that risk in the stock market is viewed by the minute and the hour, and this can be misleading for a long-term investor. When viewed from a distance over a much longer period of time, risk looks very different. In fact, volatility isn't the critical component affecting the client overall. The real concern is whether a client will have the money to meet real future needs such as retirement. When the dimension of time is added, a completely different perspective on risk comes into play.

You may have seen time charts showing stock market volatility over 3-, 5-, 10-, and 20-year periods. The farther along on the time line, the more dramatic the lessening of risk. In fact, in 10 years downside volatility almost disappears. If people would look at stock market risk the way they view their personal homes—over the long term—they would see that they're rewarded for holding their positions.

If a person has a long period of time in which to accumulate wealth, he or she should be encouraged to take risk because it will pay off. Obviously, most people don't buy a diversified portfolio of homes; they buy only one. In stock market parlance that would be considered a lot of risk, but given the fact that most homeowners plan to live in their homes a long time, that investment is not viewed as risky.

The combination of these factors—investors' emotional risk, the loss principle, and risk tolerance—should be recorded in a client's investment policy statement. The investment policy statement is a written document that outlines the rules for making investment management decisions. This should not just be an analytic document; it also should outline the amount of risk the investor has signed up for and agrees to. This is one way to make sure that the investor and the advisor are on the same page from day 1.

Our focus in this chapter has been more on the behavioral side of risk than on the analytical side. The next few chapters will walk you through how to mitigate risk while improving investment returns. As we move into Part II, the segment on wealth accumulation, we will explore advisors' opinions and use of specific investments.

3

DIVERSIFICATION AND ASSET ALLOCATION

MOST FINANCIAL ADVISORS BELIEVE that diversification is the underlying principal in achieving consistent returns and thus retiring comfortably. There are others who feel that diversification is a means of achieving mediocrity. Who is right? The final answer to that question probably will never be decided.

Historical data have largely pointed to the success of a diversified portfolio over a portfolio with little or no diversification or worse yet, a portfolio that is market-timed. Most of the information one reads that pertains to market timers is quite humorous. You may have seen brochures for timing services that chart the growth of the S&P 500 and highlight low points and high points, describing the benefits of being able to move between cash and equities to maximize an investor's performance during those swings in prices.

A study conducted by Gary Brinson, Randolph Hood, and Gilbert Beebower in 1986 analyzed the performance variations of 91 large pension funds.[1] Their report analyzed the three primary investment strategies that determine variations in portfolio performance: market timing, security selection, and asset allocation. What the study discovered was that the two strategies that had the least impact on performance variation are market timing and security selection. Market timing and security selection activities rely on attempting to predict the future. Most of Wall Street's recommendations are based on these two strategies. Wall Street firms spend billions of dollars each year trying to outguess their competition in these two areas, but the study found that 94 percent of returns came from asset allocation, as you can see below.

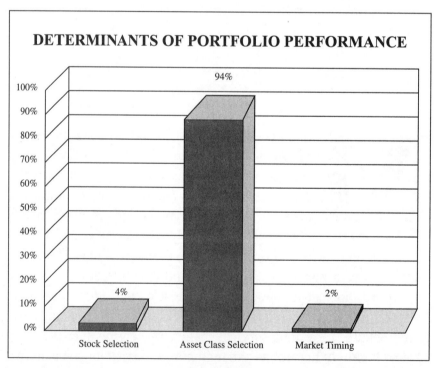

[1]Gary P. Brinson, L. Randolph Hood, and Gilbert L. Beebower, "Determinants of Portfolio Performance," *Financial Analysis Journal,* July–August 1986, pp. 39–44.

Let's look at the insights from our wealth makers and see why different advisors feel differently about the diversification dilemma so that you can make an informed decision in terms of your own investment methodology.

TO WHAT EXTENT CAN DIVERSIFICATION HELP REDUCE RISK?

Glenn Kautt says that diversification is absolutely necessary to reduce risk. Studies have shown that approximately 90 percent of individual investment risk is eliminated when a portfolio contains 20 different investments. Most investors, whether using stock or mutual funds, fail to analyze the underlying type of assets or businesses represented by our investment. As a result, many seemingly different mutual funds or even individual stocks are really operating in the same industries. If a portfolio has significant covariance in its investments (separate investments react the same way to different economic and financial stimuli), a "diversified" portfolio really isn't diversified! Improper diversification can actually hurt overall performance and dramatically increase investment risk.

Harold Evensky says, "Diversify at a minimum between fixed income and equity. The next stage would be to diversify fixed income by duration (short and intermediate—we do not use long term or low quality). First stage equity diversification would be domestic large and small and international. The next stage would be to add style diversification and emerging markets. In addition, we believe in diversifying active managers within a style or class."

John Bowen, Jr., is also a big believer in diversification: "The market does not reward investors for taking specific risks. It is easy to diversify away the specific risk of any individual stock by having many issues." Bowen's clients are broadly diversified across many countries and individual issues to include large, small, international, domestic, and value stocks.

Douglas Baker, like many advisors, believes in diversification and applies the concept of asset allocation. A typical portfolio may have six to eight categories, usually with one mutual fund for each classification. He may "split fund" a category if 20 percent of the total is within one category (the maximum he would allocate) or if current market conditions warrant a split between two styles, such as growth and value. Diversification should be universally accepted as the first commandment of money management.

Marilyn Bergen is another strong believer in diversification: "I have never found evidence to suggest that any one person or firm can consistently time the market or choose the asset category that will outperform all others for any specified period of time. Most of the historical investment experience points to diversification as a risk reduction tool."

She recommends diversification for clients both in the total portfolio by using multiple asset classes and within asset classes by using either mutual funds or a wide variety of stocks or bonds. In the fixed-income side of a portfolio she will typically use three to four asset categories. Most commonly these categories include cash equivalents, short-term U.S. bonds, intermediate-term U.S. bonds, and international bonds. In the equity side she typically uses four to five asset categories, including large and small U.S. stocks, large and small international stocks, and real estate.

Within equity categories she further diversifies by including a portion of both growth and value positions. Evidence suggests that over extended periods, value stocks outperform growth stocks. Because growth and value tend to outperform each other in cycles, Marilyn includes both types of positions if possible. Within fixed-income categories, she sometimes diversifies between government, high-grade corporate, and high-yield corporate instruments.

Thomas Muldowney agrees that there is no single mechanism that can predict any single investment or any single asset class that will advance more than all others with any degree of confidence: "It is always easy to identify the winner—just after it happened. It is simply not possible to do so with anything more than 50 percent confidence in advance."

Finally, Kim Foss-Erickson says, "The true measure of diversification is how negatively correlated investments are with one another over time. When one asset class is rising in value, the other is declining. Investments that are different but move in the same direction will tend to increase the risk and reduce the predictability of returns for the portfolio."

All the advisors I interviewed believe that at least some degree of diversification is necessary to increase the probability of consistent growth. The downside that an investor has to be cognizant of is that with diversification often come periods of market underperformance. If you are properly diversified, you probably will underperform the market when it is setting daily records as in the U.S. markets in 1998 and 1999, but in years such as 1973 and 1974, you probably will outperform the market if you define the market as U.S. large company stocks.

WHEN DO YOU DO ASSET ALLOCATION?

Wayne Caldwell explains his strategies and at the same time puts diversification into perspective: "Diversification is not a function of having many investments. A stock portfolio with 100 securities will not reduce systematic risk to the portfolio over one with only 20 securities spread across various asset classes. Older people often have too many of their assets in low-risk investments and deprive themselves of the capital growth necessary to keep up with inflation and taxes. Younger people tend to put too much money in speculative investments.

"Once assets are allocated properly for a person's financial objectives, diversification begins within those allocations. Not only should assets be diversified, strategies should as well. Dollar cost averaging is ideal for young people who are trying to build an estate, but for someone who is looking to preserve capital, there are much better strategies."

The way Wayne maximizes diversification is relatively simple. He wants his clients to participate in the returns of the great blue chip companies in the United States that are well represented by stocks in the S&P 500. To minimize decisions and errors and because 75 percent of the active managers who attempt to beat the market perform below the S&P 500 as a group, Wayne buys the entire S&P 500. He has then maximized diversification within this asset class of stocks, kept turnover low, created a tax-efficient strategy, and reduced costs. He's not concerned if a particular manager leaves and takes her supposed expertise at picking stocks with her because the clients hold all 500 stocks.

Wayne says, "If you want more return and can tolerate somewhat more risk, simply add more stocks to your portfolio as opposed to bonds." In this strategy, he uses bonds to dampen the ups and downs: "You're not going to get more return with bonds, but you'll get less risk." Within the bond portfolio, he uses short-term, high quality, and primarily U.S. government bonds. He also blends in foreign government bonds and one-year cash equivalents.

When Wayne moves to the stock component, other important portfolio risk and return factors, such as value and size, come into play: "Value companies have a higher risk and return characteristic than do growth companies. The S&P 500 primarily represents growth companies. Value companies tend to move up and down somewhat differently than do growth companies. With this difference in the movements, value stocks help offset the ups and downs in the bonds and the S&P 500. We have a higher return expectation with a higher risk expectation in the large U.S. value stocks. Stocks add to the return of bonds, and they have effective diversification because of different price movements. Value companies add to the diversification of growth stocks and bonds to create greater effective diversification.

"Another factor that adds to the risk and return of a portfolio is the size of companies. We can add small companies into the mix and develop greater return and diversification and therefore risk protection. Among small companies, growth and value companies move differently, and so you want U.S. small growth and U.S. small value companies in the portfolio.

"We also want to participate in emerging economies that are rapidly expanding toward developed status. One of the newest asset classes, created about 10 years ago, is emerging markets."

In each one of these groups Wayne buys all the stocks that fit a particular set of parameters until he has a fully diversified asset-allocated portfolio of approximately 10 different asset classes. Three of them are fixed: cash, U.S. government bonds, and foreign bonds. These classes are blended into a portfolio with U.S. large growth companies (S&P 500), U.S. large value companies, U.S. small growth companies, U.S. small value companies, international large value, international small value, and emerging markets.

Wayne states, "A process using computer models, technically called *optimization,* takes the risk and return characteristics of each asset class and incorporates them into a portfolio that has a lower risk and a higher return profile than any single asset class. This is an often overlooked but incredibly important portfolio design element.

"Another important component is a review each January of the portfolios, cash positions, new monies, or funds that need to be distributed. We use this opportunity to rebalance the portfolio. This is very critical and sometimes difficult for clients to understand. Each year we're buying the worst-performing asset class, and if we need to sell, we sell from the best-performing asset class."

If new money comes in, Wayne puts more of that money in the "dogs" from the previous year and less or no money into last year's "winner." "By systematically and unemotionally rebalancing back to the percentages of our original allocation, we are automatically selling high and buying low. In reality, we sell as infrequently as possible to control taxes," he explains.

Wayne has created a simple, elegant portfolio design that's diversified with more than 7,000 stocks spread over 10 primary asset classes. All the unintelligible "black box" strategies are removed. He has a simple explanation: He wants to participate in the returns of all the different companies and economies around the world for the rest of the client's lifetime. Wayne believes fundamentally that the human drive to do better for oneself is reflected in individual companies' successes and overall economic success over long periods. Strong academic research backs up this strategy, and very simple, straightforward fine-tuning allows maximum flexibility over the lifetime of the client.

Wayne has developed the following set of rules after years of trying everything under the sun to create the best possible results for his clients:

Rule 1.   Simple and explainable is better.

Rule 2.   Efficiency in investment portfolios, investment decisions, and long-term investment success is desirable and attainable.

Rule 3.   Use academic research as a basis for decisions, not Wall Street hype.

Rule 4.   The basic rules of investment success rarely change and will last a lifetime.

Rule 5.   Historical performance tracking is of very little help in recognizing future returns, and chasing performance creates more problems than it solves.

Rule 6.   Walk away from any advisor or strategy that even hints that human predictions are a component of success.

Rule 7.   Diversification and asset allocation are the two most important elements. Maximize the use of them in a portfolio.

Rule 8.   Use as long a time line as possible, preferably the rest of one's life.

Rule 9.   Understand that you will have a strong emotional response to the world of investing. Acknowledge your feelings, but learn to control your investor behavior.

Rule 10. Diligently seek out and develop a long-term relationship with a trusted advisor and the advisor's firm to help you stay the course and remind you of these rules.

As Wayne explains, "Adherence to these rules will dramatically increase the likelihood of achieving lifelong investment success within the context of creating financial peace of mind."

As we conclude this chapter, we can surmise that the majority of our experts agree that diversification is a fundamental principle for long-term investing. We also have a better understanding that asset allocation is not based only on a study by Brinson, Hood, and Beebower but has been proved in real life to be successful for the top advisors in the country.

INVESTMENT NOISE

DURING OUR DISCUSSIONS with advisors, an interesting term kept coming up: *investment noise.* This concept intrigued me to the point where I decided to dedicate a chapter to gaining a better understanding what investment noise is. This chapter will focus on the feedback received from our expert of experts on this topic, John J. Bowen, Jr., who has written a number of articles and three books on the subject.

Bowen believes that the vast majority of individual investors are noise investors without knowing it. His primary goal is to help his clients become *informational* investors who understand how markets work and how to apply that understanding so that they do not fall prey to the same costly mistakes that plague *noise* investors.

Bowen explains, "Noise investors believe that by regularly reading the many financial publications they can become *insiders* in regard to information that gives them some advantage. In our office we refer to this material as *investment pornography.* It gets investors all excited and confused. Not surprisingly, most noise investors significantly *under*perform the market."

Bowen demonstrates how investment noise causes confusion: "First, many of the consumer-oriented financial magazines sell the hot mutual funds—the ones with the best performance or track record. They tell their readers that these investments are the best because of what they did last week. The problem is that the likelihood of those hot funds continuing their performance is almost nil.

"What most writers of these magazines don't realize is that mutual fund managers' main goal is to raise more money. These managers tend to focus on stock selection and/or market timing, in essence, making bets. Unfortunately, these management strategies are costly to implement, have an extremely low probability of success, and are ineffective in adding value. In fact, these strategies contribute less than 6 percent of a portfolio's profit determination. Academic studies have found that 94 percent of returns are generated from making the right asset allocation decisions." (This is evidenced in the previous chart and the study by Brinson, Hood, and Beebower.)

John uses the following matrix to illustrate this point, which he first learned from Roger Gibson, the author of *Asset Allocation.* This matrix classifies investors according to what they believe will be effective in adding value. Identify the quadrant in which you currently fit. Our goal in this chapter is to move you into the quadrant that ensures the highest probability of consistent success.

Quadrant 1 is composed of investors who believe that both market timing and fundamental analysis are effective. They believe that they or others can uncover stocks or mutual funds that are mispriced and then exploit the mispricing. They want to believe that there are financial gurus who can accurately predict when the market will go up or down. People also believe that a knowledgeable stockbroker

		Market Timing	
		Yes	No
Stock or Mutual Fund Selection	Yes	1	2
	No	3	4

can pick stocks by doing research to determine the right individual security or mutual fund. Most of the public is in this quadrant, and the media play to this kind of thinking. The reality is that these methods mostly fail to deliver even market returns.

Quadrant 2 includes most people in the financial services industry. They have the experience to know that they can't predict broad market swings. However, because they have access to hundreds of market analysts, they believe they can uncover the one investment option that isn't fairly priced and thus extract value for the investor. Unfortunately, as un-American as it seems, this methodology appears on average to add no value after cost for investors.

Quadrant 3 is the tactical allocation quadrant. Investors in this quadrant believe that even though individual securities and mutual funds are efficient, somehow they, and only they, can see broad mispricing in major sectors of the market. They believe they can exploit this undervalued sector by purchasing it and then waiting for the market to finally recognize its mistake and fully value the sector.

Quadrant 4 is where most of the academic community resides. This is where you will find the informational investors. These men and women dispassionately research what works and what does not work. Academic studies indicate that the average risk premium return from active management is negative rather than positive after cost.

The reality is that people *want* to believe in gurus, market timing, stock selection, and mutual funds—Quadrant 1. However, there is no evidence that gurus exist. A real-life example was all the hoopla over the "Beardstown ladies" and their best-selling book, the *Common-Sense Investment Guide—How We Beat the Stock Market and How You Can Too*. The ladies were invited around the world to promote their stunning success and winning strategies. Then, in 1998, four years after the release of their book, an editor at *Chicago* magazine blew the lid off their story.

It turns out that a terrible mistake had been made in the calculations. The ladies hadn't really earned 13.4 percent annually over 10 years, the number emblazoned on the cover of the book and repeated on virtually every one of their television appearances and in every article about them. They hadn't beaten the market by 8.5 percentage points a year. In reality, their annual returns over that period were a mere 9.1 percent, far short of the S&P 500's 14.9 percent.

Gurus don't exist—at least, not for long!

So what are the three likely outcomes if, as in Quadrant 1, you hope to outperform the market? The best possible outcome is that you *will outperform* the market. If you do, you're happy for a while, but you expect even greater success next year. What's the likelihood that you will outperform the market by a bigger margin next year? In 1999, 86 percent of U.S. large cap mutual fund money managers didn't keep up with the past strategy of the Standard & Poor 500. In the last 10 years, 84 percent of mutual fund managers didn't keep up.

If you don't outperform the market, a second possible outcome is that you will *equal* the market. In this case you're going to be disappointed. Even if you consistently equal the market, you're not happy. Your expectations were that you were going to beat it; the writers told you that you could.

The third outcome is that you *underperform* the market. If you're a stockbroker, you're likely to be fired quickly. What's the likelihood that you will underperform the market? The likelihood is well over 50 percent that you're going to underperform the market, net after costs.

To be consistently successful, you have no choice but to follow the strategy of Quadrant 4. Become an informational investor. Don't get caught up in the noise.

The academic evidence suggests that three of the four quadrants don't add value on average. Indeed, all evidence clearly illustrates that markets are extremely efficient. The more you review the academic research, the more convinced you become.

One of the most liberating experiences is to move from noise investing to information investing. You start looking at publications and other financial reporting media differently. You begin to recognize the noise and no longer look for investment advice in media communications. If you do read the publications or watch television, it is for entertainment only.

By the way, noise investors do generate value: They create liquidity for informational investors!

5

MANAGING
PERFORMANCE
EXPECTATION

THIS MAY BE THE ONE OF THE MOST IMPORTANT CHAP-
TERS in the book, not because we're going to enlighten
you with a new investment method but because it will
give you a solid idea of what you can expect from varying investment objectives. It is very common for people to abandon their investment plans because of disappointment.
Ten years ago the benchmark rate that was used to estimate the
growth of a client's account was 8 percent. Today I see projections in
financial plans at 10, 12, and up to 16 percent! During the bull market of the 1990s certain asset classes, such as U.S. equities, performed in excess of 15 percent on average every year. It is easy to
become blind to the reality that markets are risky and tend to fluctuate. It is even possible that this year could witness a 25 to 30 percent

drop in stock prices across the board. Do I believe that will happen? No. But the idea is that you should be prepared for the worst when you set out to accumulate wealth. If you are told or believe that you can accumulate wealth at double-digit performance rates with little risk, the day you lose 10 percent is the day you will run for the hills. This is why I believe that managing performance expectations is a critical component of wealth building.

To examine the management of expectations, I first wanted to explore with our experts the common theory that with research, an investor can predict market movement. I asked the experts, "Do you see patterns in the market?"

Harold Evensky laughed. "Yes—up ... and down!" Beyond that, he believes that the market is a chaotic system and has yet to figure out how to convert that belief into a rational decision-making process. Harold has looked at neural nets and fuzzy logic, but that seems to be beyond everyone's ability. In other words, everyone sees patterns in the rearview mirror, but one must always remember that hindsight is 20/20.

Lynn Hopewell said there are plenty of patterns in the market but agrees with Harold that the trouble is that "they are not predictable." He keeps an eye on major economic indicators, but only so that he can explain what has happened, not what will happen.

Ray Ferrara also sees patterns and offers a prediction: "We are in an incredible bull market that has been fueled by unprecedented capital spending. As long as we can continue to import deflation from foreign countries (cheap labor and products), you should see this boom continue. When non-U.S. economies start to recover and grow, we may see our bull market slow down and rest for a while."

Glenn Kautt says that the overall investment markets worldwide are sensitive to several major influences: inflation, balance of payments (seen in trade deficits or surpluses), employment patterns, government intervention in the form of monetary and tax policies, and international political situations, including armed conflicts. Glenn monitors information and statistics relating to these influences regularly: "Even when regularly monitored, it is impossible to forecast or predict accurately the timing, direction, or magnitude of these influences beyond a month or two in the future. "As a result, he models his portfolios' future performances by using guidelines developed by outside research firms such as Callan and Associates: "Price fluctuations in equity and fixed-yield markets are a result of a combination of these influences. Variations can be summarized by the standard deviation of the prices of the markets or sectors."

Glenn says he also has developed probabilistic models that include these uncertainties. When these models are coupled with the uncertainties of a client's financial situation, he can predict the probability of a future financial situation. By presenting a range of outcomes rather than a single or stochastic projection, he is able to better meet the needs of a client. Why is this the case? "If a client understands the probability of a particular outcome of a retirement program, it helps us develop the client's financial plan and investment policy."

Kelley Schubert agrees that there are always patterns in the market and that the questions an investor should ask are, "Is this pattern predictable for the future?" and "What are the consequences if I am wrong?" Kelley's opinion is that trying to benefit from perceived patterns in the market is a difficult game to win: "It requires increased trading costs, a probable loss in tax efficiency, and an increased margin for error. Overcoming these obstacles means you must not only outperform a passive or index strategy, you must do so by a great margin to make up for the additional costs you have incurred."

Wayne Caldwell says that most patterns are unpredictable and do not provide any useful advantage in terms of the long-term success of an investment portfolio. "There are two important patterns that will assist clients in their long-term investment success. The first pattern is that the market will continue to have unpredictable short-term ups and downs that will be well reported in the media. The second pattern is the long-term rising trend of the world's stock markets. The key to investment success is for clients to accept the short-term ups and downs as a normal part of a successful long-term investment strategy and stay emotionally and intellectually focused on the long-term rise of the equity markets."

Lance Pelky ended this part of the discussion stating that "75 percent of the U.S. workforce consists of people between the ages of 39 and 53 (baby boomers). They are in their peak earning, spending, and investment years. The chairman of the Federal Reserve or events such as Y2K may sway public opinion for a while, but the *current will go where it wants to go.* When you couple the technology explosion with a force such as the baby boomers, you have something very big that you don't want to miss. You must systematically invest in long-term trends."

That is interesting feedback. Basically all the experts say that it is difficult even for chartists to predict the future on the basis of past results. I personally learned a lesson about this topic during the last three years. I listened to world-renowned professors Ken French and Eugene Fama discuss the benefit of buying mutual funds with a value style. I used a software program to compare the historical track record of value stocks versus growth stocks for five-year holding periods. In almost every case the value stocks outperformed the growth stocks and did so by a large margin. I naturally invested in the value stocks and for the last three years have greatly underperformed the growth stocks. When Ken French was asked why this was happening, he offered the simple explanation that "investment performance is random." There will be periods of time when value outperforms growth and vice versa. I just happened to buy value when it was randomly out of favor. The idea is that I have to hold the funds longer than three years to realize the potential payoff of value stocks. Without this explanation, it would have been easy to ditch the value funds and buy growth funds. That is where people tend to lose. In all likelihood, I would buy the growth stocks just as the value stocks returned to favor. The conclusion I draw is to diversify and stay the course.

But let's go one step further. It appears that clients/consumers are rarely satisfied with their returns. It seems that clients seldom feel successful. Therefore, I asked the experts, "What has to happen for your clients to be considered successful investors?"

Lynn Hopewell feels that his clients have to see there are ways to accomplish their objectives. He regularly revisits their goals and objectives to verify that they are on track. They have to keep the long-term viewpoint and not succumb to short-term market volatility.

Ray Ferrara had the following success rules for his clients:

1.   They have a sense of well-being that comes from knowing that come what may, they and their families are financially and emotionally able to achieve their hopes and dreams.

2.   Their investment, estate, and tax-planning goals are in the process of being realized or have already been attained within acceptable risk-tolerance levels.

3.   They have a risk-management strategy (insurance, etc.) in place that is appropriate and cost-effective.

Glenn Kautt believes a successful client relationship is one in which the client and he both understand and agree on the client's financial and personal goals. Once Glenn has agreement, he maintains success by working to provide performance that gives clients the financial resources to meet their personal goals.

John Bowen, Jr., provided us with an interesting quote: Success is having what you want, and happiness is being satisfied with what you have." He explains: "For clients to truly be successful, they need to know what they want. A key part of our wealth management process is to help them understand what their financial goals are. Once they are aware of those goals, they have a personal benchmark with which to measure their success. Success is therefore obtaining your defined personal financial goals."

Douglas Baker believes success is achieved when funds bring about a reasonably defined rate of return or, in the case of a retiree, provide a predefined lifestyle free from the lack of sleep caused by financial uncertainty. However, neither the amount in the portfolio nor the rate of return necessarily brings the feeling of success without clients first defining their objectives.

Floyd Shilanski sums it up this way, "They achieve their dreams, not mine, whether that is debt reduction, getting control of their finances, just getting started, or wealth accumulation."

2

WEALTH ACCUMULATION

Your success in accumulating wealth can be influenced strongly by the types of investments you choose, how much you pay for those investments, and how frequently you change your mind. In this section you will hear the experts' opinions on the pros and cons of accumulating wealth through company stock options, E-trading, market timing, mutual fund selection, and separate account management—an investment method that is growing rapidly in popularity.

6

MARKET TIMING

MARKET TIMERS WOULD LIKE INVESTORS TO BELIEVE that they can predict market peaks and valleys. They preach how transferring between cash and equities during these peaks and valleys can lead to unbelievable returns and rapid growth. However, my opinion has always been that in most cases you will do better if you buy an equity fund that they use for timing and just hold on to it.

Before we jump into the opinions of our experts on market timing specifically, let's first look at the differences between random selection and strategic selection. I asked the experts to share any information or details about how their selection systems outperform the dartboard mentality.

Lynn Hopewell begins the discussion with an interesting clarification: "In the area of securities selection, we never claim to do any better than the market for any particular asset class. However, the dartboard implies a mindless technique that is implemented with indexes."

Lynn doesn't use index funds; he uses asset class funds. These funds are typically very passive, but they do not just randomly choose stocks. Lynn explains that "the dartboard approach alone is inadequate because securities selection is not where the problems are in investing; many times it is how long one holds the investment."

Mark Sumsion explains that a fund selection is far more important than market timing: "Knowing when to use market timing and when *not* to is the key most investors never really discover. Market timing in a healthy market can cause an investor to reduce returns by being out of the market at the wrong time, but the buy-and-hold approach in an unhealthy market can cause an investor to realize substantial losses. Therefore, it is critical to understand market cycles."

Mark believes unhealthy markets are caused when the Federal Reserve begins to drain money or liquidity from the economy: "At some point this begins to hurt corporate earnings by starving the economy of the fuel it needs to grow. The rate of decline of the growth of the M2, combined with a rising interest rate environment, will cause the value of long-term bonds to fall and the U.S. dollar to decline. This in turn will hurt stocks by creating either a bear market or a sideways whipsaw trader's market where very little progress is made.

"It is the degree by which the Federal Reserve attempts to control the economy that will determine the degree of an economic contraction. When the Federal Reserve begins to move against the economy, it is time to use market timing, as risk is building. Investors can obtain this information from the Federal Reserve Bank of St. Louis on the Internet at http://www.stls.frb.org-images-publications/usfd/page8.gif.

"This will show an investor the direction of the money supply and the degree of growth. To fine-tune the market's underlying health you need some good technical tools. We monitor a variety of breadth indicators to measure the strength or weakness of the market, such as the ratio of how many stocks are making new lows for the year relative to new highs, advance-decline lines, McClellan Summation Index oscillators, and the like. To forecast trend changes, we use 'detrended' stochastics, which measure overbought and oversold market conditions."

Kelley Schubert suggests that since throwing darts is a random selection method, so will be the errors encountered: "I use a fully diversified, passive investment approach that emphasizes indexing different risk dimensions of the equity markets. Everyone knows that 'the higher the risk, the higher the return.' The only risks that are wise to take are those for which one gets compensated. Many of the risk elements in the market can be eliminated with proper diversification, meaning that you can achieve the long-term rate of return without the short-term risk. A dartboard mentality would lend itself to a certain level of diversified risk and would therefore, be an inferior approach to use."

Neither Lynn nor Kelley is a market timer, but both believe that an investor has to be more strategic than just randomly picking stocks.

John Bowen, Jr., thinks using a dartboard is fine if you're only choosing a few stocks: "Even though it's random, you still have a specific risk of being poorly diversified." His average portfolio is in 25 different countries with over 8,000 individual securities, effectively eliminating the specific risk.

Wayne Caldwell thinks that a randomly selected group of stocks from the New York Stock Exchange is likely to outperform the careful selection of active money managers. As was previously discussed, the key to adding value to an investor's long-term portfolio is the understanding that one can segment the U.S. market as well as international markets into groups of stocks that respond differently in economic cycles and have different risk and reward characteristics.

DO YOU TRADE STOCKS FREQUENTLY OR EVER ATTEMPT TO TIME THE MARKET?

Lynn Hopewell response is a big "No! It just runs up costs." Lynn tells clients that the better a job he does selecting managers, the less often he has to change them.

Glenn Kautt also says absolutely not and cites studies that have shown that more frequent trading simply produces larger trading costs and a poorer long-term performance. Kautt says market timing for large portfolios is a joke. "No one has been able to consistently deliver controlled risk, increased performance, and lower costs to investors by using market timing."

Douglas Baker believes that market conditions dictate the frequency of trade. Baker traded more frequently in 1999 than in any other year in the last 20. "This was in response to shifting sectors where we moved from financials, health, and bonds into other sectors, including money market funds. Also, as many funds come out of the closet and are defined by holdings, changes have occurred.

"An example was a fund classified as small cap, when in fact the majority of its holdings were in technology. Small cap perhaps, but really a 'closet' technology fund. Issues of how to define growth versus value have also caused changes." Doug's preference is to find a good fund manager and stay the course, but "that's been difficult lately."

Wayne Caldwell says, "In a perfect world I wouldn't trade at all except to provide clients with income, and then I would utilize more favorable long-term capital gains to create that income. A fundamental problem with the entire investment industry is that it trades excessively to the detriment of the clients, relative to both their investment returns and their returns after taxes."

In conclusion, market timing by a diverse group of financial advisors appears to be a major faux pas. I find this gratifying since I have always believed that the hype of timing is more a sales gimmick than an achieved reality. One must understand that market timing is growing as a way of investing and beware of the pitfalls.

7

MUTUAL FUND SELECTION

S INCE YOU PAY AN ADVISOR largely to build a portfolio that meets your risk tolerance and long-term financial objectives, it is extremely important to know how advisors choose the funds they use. Some advisors select funds by using basic criteria such as past performance or Morningstar ratings; others take a very technical approach and study exposure distribution, alpha, beta, the Sharpe ratio, correlation coefficients, and additional criteria. You will find that this chapter is a bit lengthy but very important.

First, let's take a step back and briefly describe how mutual funds work. The manager of a mutual fund uses a pool of capital to buy a variety of stocks, bonds, or money market instruments to meet the advertised financial objectives of the fund. These objectives cover a wide range. Some funds follow aggressive policies, involving greater risk in search of higher returns; others seek current income and little risk.

When you purchase "no-load" mutual fund shares, you pay net asset value (NAV), which is the value of a fund's total investment minus any debt, divided by the number of outstanding shares. For example, if the fund's investment value is $26,000, it has no debt, and there are 1000 shares outstanding, the NAV is $26 per share. The NAV is not a fixed figure because it must reflect the daily changes in the price of the securities in the fund's portfolio.

Sales charges ("loads") are commissions paid on the sale of mutual funds. Commissions used to be charged up front, otherwise known as A-shares, but that's changed. There are now several ways for mutual fund companies to charge fees. Some sales charges, as in B-shares, are levied on the back end as a contingent deferred sales charge. The load is charged when the investor redeems shares in the fund. A customer who redeems shares in the first year of ownership typically pays a 5 percent sales charge. The sales charge drops by an equal amount each year. After six years the shares can be redeemed without a further charge. While there are no front-end charges, these funds often have higher internal costs.

C-shares pay the selling broker up to 1 percent per year based on assets. This fee comes directly from investment performance and is paid to the selling broker. C-shares may have no up-front fee, possibly a 1 percent deferred sales charge in year 1 (sometimes longer), and higher annual expenses (up to 1 percent extra per year).

No-load mutual funds do *not* mean *no cost*. Some no-load funds charge a redemption fee of 1 to 2 percent of the NAV of the shares to cover expenses incurred mainly through advertising or to avoid market timing. Fee comparisons are particularly important. Every dollar charged comes directly from the performance of the fund. Remember to compare the proverbial apples to apples, in this case similar equities to equity funds, and similar bonds to bond funds.

Fees paid for the operational costs of running a fund may include employees' salaries, marketing and publicity, costs servicing the toll-free phone line, printing and mailing published materials, computers for tracking investments and account balances, and accounting fees. A fund's operating expenses are quoted as a percentage of the investment; the percentage represents an annual fee or charge. An investor can find this number in a fund's prospectus in the fund expenses section, entitled "Total Fund Operating Expenses" or "Other Expenses."

A mutual fund's operating expenses are normally invisible to investors because they're deducted before any return is paid, and they are automatically charged on a daily basis. Beware, though: A subaccount can have a very low management fee but have exorbitant operating expenses. A fund that trades frequently will have more wire charges, for instance, than will a fund that does not.

A fund's transaction costs (or the cost of buying and selling stocks) have three components: (1) the actual dollars paid in commissions, (2) the market impact, or the impact a manager's trade has on the market price for the stock (this varies with the size of the trade and the skill of the trader), and (3) the opportunity cost of the return (positive or negative) given up by not executing the trade instantaneously.

For example, when an individual investor places an order to buy 300 shares of a $30 stock (a $9000 investment), he or she is likely to get a commission bill for about $204, or 2.3 percent of the value of the investment. Even at a discount broker, commissions are likely to cost between $82 (0.9 percent) and $107 (1.2 percent). A mutual fund, by comparison, is more likely to buy 30,000 to 300,000 shares at a time! Its commission costs often run in the vicinity of one-tenth of the commission an investor would pay at a discount broker. Where a commission might have been $0.35 a share, the mutual fund could pay only $0.05 a share or even less. The commission savings can (and should) mean higher returns for you as a mutual fund shareholder.

Now that you have a thorough understanding of mutual funds, let's look at our advisors' methods for fund selection. Let's face it, the star rating by Morningstar is somewhat meaningless for choosing a hot fund since it is a hindsight look. The good news is that you should not be looking for a hot fund. Consistency is more important than one good year. Star ratings are important to get an idea of who did well last year, but look beyond them and see how a fund has done over the last 3 to 5 and 10 years.

HOW DO YOU ANALYZE AND SELECT MUTUAL FUNDS?

Mark Sumsion's first step is to create a family of funds and then begin a selection culling process. He uses funds no-transaction-fee based (NTF) funds at Fidelity, which represents hundreds and hundreds of different no-load mutual funds.

Then he divides the mutual funds according to volatility. Standard deviations, betas, and other tools will reveal which funds are aggressive, moderate, and conservative. These funds are then placed within a family according to a certain "financial speed."

The computer then analyzes each of the funds according to its relative strength and ranks all the funds within each family class from the strongest down to the weakest in relative performance. The strongest mutual funds are the buy candidates. Mark then begins to investigate the buy candidates: How big is the fund? Are there any up-front load charges or back-end costs? Are there any penalties, charges, or minimum holding periods if the investment is liquidated in a hurry? What are the investment philosophy and style? How well is the fund performing compared to an appropriate benchmark, such as the S&P 500 or Nasdaq 100 or a more conservative benchmark such as the 30-year Treasury bond? This narrows the buy candidates further until the cream rises to the surface.

The next step is market analysis: Is the market healthy or not? How long do we think the fundamentals will support a positive upward trend? Are large cap funds stronger than small cap funds? Which sectors are the strongest? Is the Nasdaq stronger than the S&P 500? How well is our buy candidate behaving in the current market environment? Is it beating the market or underperforming for short-, intermediate-, and long-term periods?

Once funds have been selected and bought, the fourth step begins: monitoring a fund's performance. If a fund falls in its relative strength performance, a trade-up develops where assets are sold or placed into stronger performers. In a healthy market Mark's objective is to be invested in those funds that show the strongest momentum.

Patrick Moran looks at long-term track records and seeks established fund companies. This is pretty basic and is a good place to start.

Joe Campisi uses Datamax, Standard & Poor's, and honest recommendations from portfolio managers. This is yet another fundamental that represents a good build on Patrick's advice.

Glenn Kautt uses both retail and institutional mutual funds. He does this to lower trading and management costs. He analyzes funds and managers by using a rigorous proprietary 35-step screening process. For example, he has screening criteria for managers, overall performance, and performance relative to the fund's sector, costs, size and maturity, and style drift.

Marilyn Bergen also uses mutual funds to a large extent in client portfolios. She has a fairly lengthy process for analyzing funds: "It starts with our initial screen, which includes the following information: (a) performance over year-to-date, 1, 3, 5, and 10 years compared to the appropriate category and appropriate index, (b) alpha and Sharpe ratios compared to category averages, (c) manager tenure, and (d) expense ratios."

After the initial screen, she checks style drift, the consistency of investment type, and the amount of money in cash versus the amount being invested. In addition, for stock funds, she specifically looks at turnover ratio and exposure to large versus middle versus small versus micro cap stocks.

For bond funds, Marilyn looks at the following additional information:

- Credit quality
- Average duration
- Average maturity

- Exposure to emerging market debt
- Exposure to nonrated debt
- Exposure to exotic mortgage-backed debt

If she feel she needs additional information, she calls the fund manager or an analyst on the team to clarify issues.

Kelley Schubert primarily uses passive and index mutual funds. When selecting a mutual fund, Kelley evaluates the discipline and stability of the investment objective: "If a fund is supposed to be a small cap fund, I want it to remain a small cap fund even when small companies are out of favor. It must have a long track record of adhering to its stated investment philosophy." He also looks at operating expenses. Since he uses primarily passively managed funds, he is not willing to pay high expenses for increased trading or analysis. "Tax efficiency is huge. Low-fund turnover is a must."

Douglas Baker uses funds exclusively. His research to determine appropriate funds starts with *Morningstar, Investors Business Daily,* and other publications. The fund universe is screened by objective and category ratings, tenure of management, MPT (Modern Portfolio Theory) statistics, holdings by sector or region, and other factors. He uses only no-load or load-waived funds. The process repeats itself every month, changing the funds in use if that is warranted.

Ray Ferrara checks on a fund's *Morningstar* category rating. The fund must at least be in its category's top half for the one-, three-, and five-year periods. The fund should be in its top quartile for two of three of those periods. The fund manager should have a substantial track record covering several market corrections, not just bull markets. The fund's expenses should be low compared to those of its peers. The fund should have a beta that is consistent with its returns and should also have a strong alpha.

Thomas Muldowney wants to find the low-cost providers, single-asset-class subaccounts, diversification, low portfolio turnover, and identifiable goals. He typically requires index-based investments more or less in the following order: analogue indexes, representative indexes, quantitative/sampling indexes, virtual indexes, passive asset strategies, and disciplined investment style.

Stan Hargrave wants a positive alpha (two-thirds of returns), a disciplined philosophy, and humility and wants to see that the managers' own money is invested along with the clients'.

John Bowen, Jr., says that because of his belief in efficient markets, he attempts to identify money managers who add value not by predicting the future but by utilizing their knowledge of how markets work and reducing the cost of trading or taxes to maximize the benefit in each asset class for their clients.

As you can see, some of the systems our advisors use would be difficult for consumers to implement on their own. But what is consistent, fundamentally, is to look for established firms with good track records. From there, I recommend working with a qualified financial advisor to decipher which funds from the universe you are examining will best work for you.

SEPARATE ACCOUNT MANAGERS

ONE OF THE HOTTEST TRENDS ON THE ADVISOR SCENE is the use of separate account managers. In the past, separate account managers were only available to individuals with over $1 million to invest. Today there are firms like Lockwood Financial Securities, Inc. who now make it possible to purchase separate accounts for as little as $100,000.

Since most of our advisors do not use separate account managers, I thought it would be valuable to turn this discussion over to Len Reinhart, one of the founders of Lockwood Financial Securities, Inc.

Len explains: "Fifteen years ago we were just beginning to mention mutual funds to our clients. Back then you could easily list all of them on a few four- by five-inch index cards. You had to take time to sell the whole concept and explain how a mutual fund worked. Today there are so many funds that tracking them has become a full-time industry. Mutual funds have become household names, ex-fund managers get paid huge salaries to do TV commercials, and funds raise billions, not millions, of dollars. These days if you ask a group of average investors to explain a mutual fund, almost 95 percent will know and be able to give a good definition. Mutual funds have become the financial success story of the 1990s.

"At a recent seminar attended by attorneys and accountants, I posed a different question. I asked how many could explain what an individually managed account was. Almost no hands were raised. Although individually managed accounts have been around as long as mutual funds, the typical financial professional—CPA, insurance and estate planner, or financial planner—much less the investor, still doesn't *really* have a full grasp or understanding of individually managed accounts, how they work, or why. They are used in only a very small percentage of cases. Today there's over $7 trillion invested in mutual funds and only $300 billion in individually managed accounts.

"Our industry needs the same education process for individually managed accounts that we used for mutual funds. I believe so strongly in this concept, it's become a part of my mission and is one of the reasons why I'm in the business I'm in. Don't make the mistake of assuming that your clients or even the other financial professionals you network with understand the nuances and the differences between an individually managed account and a mutual fund. Financial professionals generally describe individually managed accounts vaguely as 'that cookie cutter or wrap-fee thing' or say it's 'a mutual fund for big clients.' They really don't know that what we have now is very different from the wrap fee programs of 10 years ago.

"Here is a short course in explaining individually managed accounts, or so-called separate account managers:

"An individually managed account has similarities to mutual funds, such as professional management, cost, diversification, and liquidity. The difference is that in a mutual fund you own shares in a company that owns a portfolio of stocks and/or bonds. In an individually managed account the portfolio manager buys securities specifically for each investor. This allows the portfolio manager to customize the portfolio and run it after tax. In a mutual fund the portfolio manager cannot take into consideration individual investor nuances. In an individually managed account you own the underlying securities in your account. The biggest difference comes on the taxable side and the customization side from a mutual fund. If you own the individual securities, you can do some things that mutual funds can't. That's both the key advantage and the difference.

"The original wrap fee of 3 percent is all unbundled now. You can buy them any way you want, feewise, but if you look at the core elements of an advisory fee, what does that mean? That's typically about 50 basis points for the smallest accounts. Money manager fees and equity accounts are generally 40 to 55 points. Brokerage costs are bundled in, typically at about 25 basis points. The reason is that if you're buying 35 to 40 securities, the client will get killed on the transaction costs. Therefore, for the core managed account, the product itself is about 125 basis points.

"On a comparable basis, the average equity mutual fund is at 140 basis points. When you throw in the brokerage costs, which Morningstar estimates at 30 basis points, you're at 170. The exact number isn't that important, but the point is that individually managed accounts are not expensive. The costs are about the same as or even less than those of a mutual fund. And the nice part about managed accounts is that there is economy of scale for the client. As the client's assets go up, the expense ratio gets cheaper.

"The capital gains realization rate (the percentage of unrealized gains that are realized each year) is 5 to 25 percent with an individually managed account. Right now it's 50 percent in the mutual fund business. Here's what happens to people and why they're waking up: A fund comes out, and it's $20 NAV. The client buys in at $30; the NAV drops to $25. There are capital gains distributions, and all of a sudden the client is looking at something he or she bought at $30, and it dropped to $25, and the client has to pay taxes on it. The system works, but the clients don't understand it. When this market turns and you witness a significant redemption, that's when you're going to see the real impact of unrealized capital gains buildup.

"The average mutual fund right now has 20 percent unrealized capital gains sitting in it. An individually managed account has none because the cost basis doesn't get established until the day the firm buys in for the client. Average portfolio turnover in an individually managed account is somewhere between 20 and 45 percent, depending on the manager. The average for a mutual fund is 88 percent. People assume that low turnover means more tax efficiency, but that is not necessarily so. My favorite response from a money manager, who was asked how he cuts his losses was, 'We don't have losses. We harvest our tax credits.'

"Many people say they don't worry about taxes, and if you have a manager who really has good total return, that will make up for the taxes. But over a five-year period of time you need 91 basis points of excess return to make up for taxes. How many managers over five years can generate 91 basis points, net alpha, over the market?

"Let's assume a 10 percent return for a mutual fund and a managed account. Over a three-year period a managed account loses about 81 basis points to taxes, whereas the typical mutual fund loses about 240 basis points. Those numbers are in line with just about every study you're going to look at on the after-tax effects of mutual funds. The average mutual fund, after tax, retains about 74 percent of the return for the client. In an individually managed account it varies between 85 and 95 percent of the total return. We generally look for managers who can retain in excess of 90 percent of their total return for the client.

"What are the issues in the real world that we're seeing and trying to solve that make individual securities work? Low-cost-basis stock holdings and a bull market. With individually managed accounts, there are managers who will assume the low-cost-basis stock and come up with three-year plans for how to liquidate and diversify it. They'll look at each individual tax lot. There may be higher-cost tax lots that they can liquidate early to start the diversification process.

"Another type of client may be somebody who owns a business or has an otherwise huge position in a specific company in an industry. There are now fulfillment managers who will work around that position. The client can't sell the business, or the stock if the client is an executive of the corporation, or the investment is in options the client can't liquidate. A manager needs to come in and run a portfolio around that with the rest of the client's money."

"In summary, I think you're going to see this area explode," Len concludes. "Not only is the press getting behind individually managed accounts, we're seeing the big players who have huge advertising budgets starting to get behind this concept. The individually managed account is the biggest thing that technology has changed in this business in the past couple of years. Technology has really enhanced efficiency and the ability to run money to an after-tax objective. I'm not being critical of mutual funds. What I'm saying is that there's another investment product here that is very similar but has different attributes, and there's a way to use it in your strategies."

THE PROCESS OF SELECTING A MONEY MANAGER

Step 1: Working with an Advisor

What needs to be known before hiring a money manager is subjective in nature and difficult to learn. All investors have individual investment requirements. Some investors have tax considerations; others do not. Some need income, while others want growth of capital. Most important, investors seek out the knowledge of experts because they believe professional managers can do a better job than they can do themselves.

These separate investment needs often cause managers to handle portfolios in different ways. The way managers choose to report on portfolios leads to different performance results. Consequently, performance numbers often say less about a manager than an investor assumes. This is where an advisor's efforts are invaluable in assessing a client's risk tolerance and objectives and finding an appropriate match in a money manager.

An advisor is necessary to help an investor do the following:

1.   Define and establish realistic investment objectives and implement
     a plan that assures the realization of those objectives. All the books
     on investing agree that an investor must have a plan but never tell
     him or her how to develop it. The best way to develop a plan is to
     have access to viable information and have someone on the other
     side of that information to interpret it properly.
2.   Develop a reasonable perspective on the overall market outlook.
3.   Select specific investments that meet the necessary criteria deter-
     mined by the investor's particular situation.
4.   Monitor overall performance against established objectives. To
     reduce risk, it is important first to determine what time period will
     be involved and then to find a money manager whose past perfor-
     mance record and individual style is most suited to the investor's
     objectives.

Step 2: Types of Money Managers

Choosing a money manager once was a simple process. The world of
investment management was the private domain of large pension
managers and bank trust departments. Selecting a manager for a pension depended more on the manager's client list than on his or her
investment track record. For individual accounts, most investors felt
bank trust departments were a safe and conservative place to keep
their money.

BANKS.   These institutions are abundant in number, existing in
virtually every community. Nearly half of all smaller pension plans
are managed by bank trust departments whose sponsors selected
them because of their own past associations with the bank. Broaden-
ing the relationship to include money management services seems
both a wise and an expedient thing to do. There may, however, be
some underlying disadvantages, one of which is that historically,
banks have had a tendency to underperform. Also, their investment
choices frequently are impeded or delayed by the need for committee
approval, which may prevent timely action. An investor looking in
from the outside may not be in a position to evaluate a bank's performance in the proper light.

It is also important to realize that a bank's trust departments generate revenue from the assets customers entrust to them and charge customers a percentage fee for taking control of their money. They are, of course, obliged to provide investors with something to do with their money, although they would just as soon provide the services connected with rolling the money over in CDs and then relend it and make more money on the spread. For people who are interested in achieving in some growth, a bank will provide money management services, primarily in order to appear accommodating. Even so, most banks are not in the money management business. Instead, they are in the business of borrowing money from an investor and lending it to somebody else at a higher price. Realistically speaking, banks are remarketers of money as opposed to money managers. Again, we must emphasize that a bank charges an investor to manage the money it is using.

BROKERAGE HOUSES.   Brokerage houses are investment management subsidiaries that represent a growing segment of the investment management market. While they certainly give individual attention to accounts and provide investment flexibility, they also have drawbacks. Perhaps the most prevalent one is the fact that their research information comes from a parent company that can be biased. In addition, securities transactions often are arranged through the parent firm, and this may result in higher trading costs.

Another point to consider: As with banks and mutual funds, how can an investor be sure that a broker is working in her or his best interest? The broker may not be doing that if he or she does not also expose the investor to outside money managers, thereby giving the investor a greater choice and an opportunity to make important comparisons.

A number of brokerage firms today are nothing short of adamant on the subject of offering only their own money management services to potential investors, choosing not to give up a portion of the fee to outside professionals. Such decisions are made by the board of directors of each individual brokerage firm, and while these firms may strongly imply that their service includes individual attention, what many offer is actually "blanket" management for everybody. Although blanket management is not necessarily a bad thing, who is in a position to say that the brokerage firms' style of money management is the right style for everyone?

You should always try to find out whether a manager has been excluded from doing business with any brokerage firms. Similarly, it helps if a manager's name is on a brokerage's approved list of managers.

INDEPENDENT INVESTMENT MANAGEMENT FIRMS. Independent investment management firms are fast becoming the largest groups that offer investment services. They provide the most flexible and complete array of personalized investment services for the intermediate-size pension sponsor. Generally, investment professionals who offer individual account management own them. Their highly competitive nature encourages them to strive for superior performance, and because these professionals tend to be well compensated, these firms experience little personnel turnover.

Back in the mid-1970s, there were a total of 2500 independent money managers; at present, the number is approaching 11,000. Banks, insurance companies, mutual funds, and brokerage firms have all been spawning grounds for their independent talent, and so they frequently are referred to as the "best of the best."

Independent money managers, the ultimate entrepreneurs, are highly motivated by the capitalistic system and therefore tend to do well for their clients and themselves. That is not to say that every single money manager is better than every brokerage firm or mutual fund, for that is hardly the case. It is the advisor's job to sift through their professional backgrounds and past performance records to properly evaluate and categorize them. After an investor has selected the "best among the best" these choices will be narrowed to those whose geographic locations are most favorable, those who have shown proficiency in larger or smaller accounts (depending on the client's specific needs), and finally those whose individual style most effectively complements the investment objective of the client. After three or four final candidates have been chosen, the consultant will help the client make an individual decision that is based in large measure on the "chemistry" that exists between the money manager and the potential client. From the standpoint of compatibility, it must be a good marriage in order for it to work well on both sides.

Step 3: The Due Diligence Process

This qualifying process, which is better known as due diligence by the investment industry, simply means that care has been taken to substantiate the suitability of a manager. How can an investor gather the necessary information?

REQUEST A COPY OF THE MANAGER'S ADV (ADVISOR REGISTRATION) FORM. No matter how impressive a manager's general marketing information is, investors should keep in mind that this information serves the purposes of the manager, not those of the investor. Disclosures usually reflect what the manager wants the investor to know. Knowledgeable investors have other ways to gather information about managers. Because the Securities and Exchange Commission (SEC) regulates investment managers, there is additional information in disclosure statements on file with the government.

The most important of these disclosure documents is the ADV. By law, a manager must provide Part II of the form (or an equivalent disclosure) to prospective clients. While Part II is the only form legally required to be furnished to the public, it never hurts to ask for both parts.

The ADV provides basic background information on a manager's state registrations, disciplinary or legal problems, ownership, potential conflicts of interest in regard to fees or commissions, and financial condition as well as the background of the firm's principals. Investors should keep in mind that the SEC never judges the merits or accuracy of the information provided in an ADV. Its purpose is to place basic information about the manager on the public record. By having an ADV, an investor has an opportunity to do some basic background checking. Obvious areas of interest are prior employment of the firm's principals and their educational backgrounds. When legal actions against a firm are discovered, investors should try to obtain copies of the court-filed complaints. By checking with the SEC's enforcement division, an investor may uncover actions taken by the SEC against a manager for regulatory violations.

THE FORM 13F FILING. If a manager handles $100 million or more in equities, SEC regulations require that a quarterly 13F filing be made. The filing states the equity positions and the number of shares held by the manager. Because the manager submits his or her portfolio positions quarterly, these reports often accurately predict the manager's performance for the coming quarter. Some managers may argue that because portfolio adjustments often occur between filings, the 13F is an inaccurate performance measure. Most managers have portfolio turnovers of about 25 percent a year or higher. Even at 40 percent turnover a year, the average quarter has only a 10 percent change in portfolio positions—a relatively small amount. This gives an investor using the 13F filing another way of comparing a manager's publicly reported performance with his or her SEC 13F filings.

MANAGERS WITH PUBLIC FUNDS. While it's more the exception than the rule, investors should always check to see whether a manager manages a mutual fund in addition to individual accounts. If the manager does this, one should compare the performance of the manager's individual composites with that of his or her mutual fund. The two should be similar in performance since it is unlikely that different investment styles are being applied to each one. Because of regulations governing mutual funds, investors are safer using the performance of the mutual fund rather than that of the manager's individual account composite.

FROM THE HORSE'S MOUTH. It is unlikely that most managers will voluntarily reveal reasons for not doing business with them. A manager's disclosure is by nature a one-sided viewpoint. There are numerous questions we could list here that would be prudent to ask a manager. For the sake of brevity, we will limit ourselves to two questions. First, it is important to understand the history of the management team. If managers have come and gone, it is important to know who they were and why they left. As in any organization, the members of a management team must work well together for the team to succeed. If there is dissension among those making the decisions, portfolio consistency may suffer.

The second question, if truthfully answered, is one of the most telling pieces of information about any manager. An investor should ask the manager to state the total asset value and the number of new accounts acquired and lost during the last five years. A good manager has little to fear from this question. On the basis of this one piece of evidence alone, most investors could save themselves much trouble.

Other factors investors might want to know are the size of the firm, how long it has been in business, its clientele list, and any referrals it may want to disclose. Common sense dictates that these basic questions be explored. Investors should be careful of firms that are growing so fast that service and performance could suffer. A faster-growing manager must devote additional time and attention to the administration of his or her business. This is sometimes detrimental to securities research and portfolio performance.

Step 4: Selection Based on Manager Styles
An investor who has enough money to hire more than one investment manager can increase her or his chance of being in the right place more than once during a complete market cycle and with lower overall volatility.

VALUE MANAGERS. The primary motivation of this type of manager is to select securities on the basis of known information. This information may take the form of price/earnings (P/E) screens or screens for various financial characteristics. In using a P/E screen, for example, P in the ratio is today's price and E is the trailing 12 months' earnings. This style frequently is associated with a strong emphasis or discipline based on the foregoing selection methods. A value manager tries to find stocks where the price is 30 to 50 percent less than breakup or replacement of the company assets.

Value managers do best after a long market decline or at the bottom of a market cycle. Also, in periods when market prices are cheaper, pessimism is very high and economic problems are very widespread. A value manager is not necessarily going to focus as much on the economy but will concentrate more on the pricing of individual securities relative to their book value or replacement costs.

RELATIVE VALUE MANAGERS.   A relative value manager looks at different sectors and tries to determine the best value in each sector. One sector might be financial, another energy, and a third consumer staples. This means that the manager may own a stock in one sector that has a much higher P/E ratio than does a stock in another sector.

Relative value managers look within a sector and do a bottom-up analysis within that sector. This may sound like a sector rotator manager looking only for values in each sector to determine which sector is going to do the best. A relative value manager does not want to be limited to one sector in case that sector goes out of favor. Relative value managers are trying to do something in between by not letting absolute value force them to be overly concentrated. They look at the relative value of stocks in each sector.

GROWTH MANAGERS.   Some people confuse growth managers with emerging growth managers. *Emerging* means it is a smaller company that is growing in size (hence the smaller capitalization), whereas *growth* stocks are companies that have earnings that are generally above average for the market.

Growth managers are more attractive in periods when the market is doing well and the companies a growth manager buys are doing the best within the market, showing very strong earnings growth. A high degree of volatility comes into play with growth managers because they manage higher-multiple stock. The P/E multiples are higher, and consequently, the volatility of the stocks is greater.

Growth managers track the growth of earnings by using a thematic approach. They identify companies, both domestically and internationally, which will take advantage of the trends that are unfolding, such as the growth of world communications, health, and international telecommunications and companies that have had good growth in these areas and are not tied to cyclical business cycles. These companies actually did exceptionally well throughout the entire recession because their stocks were moving as a result of uninterrupted earnings growth.

There are also distinctions between large cap growth managers and small-cap growth managers. There are periods in which growth stocks in the large-cap sectors do exceptionally well because there is a high level of safety, meaning higher-quality and better-capitalized companies. Unfortunately, growth stocks with smaller capitalization are overlooked to a wide extent because small- or medium-cap stocks happen to be out of vogue with the market at a particular time.

In applying an earnings growth approach, investors have to be more definitive about whether they are talking about large caps or small caps. If an investor wants to employ a value approach to earnings and large caps have already made their big move while small caps haven't and the investor is also willing to accept a higher level of volatility, perhaps smaller-cap companies will be more attractive.

EMERGING GROWTH MANAGERS.   As the name suggests, emerging growth managers tend to buy stocks that have a high degree of price volatility. This is a bottom-up style of management in that the primary motivation for buying a particular stock is inherent in the stock itself. These are the "stock pickers." Some base purchases on price momentum or earnings momentum, not only on a change in the way a company is perceived.

QUALITY GROWTH MANAGERS.   In using a hybrid Index, the primary purpose of a quality growth manager is to replicate the performance of the market. An example would be a majority, if not all, of the stocks in the upper half of the S&P 500. Many managers perform as well as the market with lower relative market risk; some perform better than the market with equivalent market risk.

BALANCE GROWTH MANAGERS.   Balance growth managers typically do not buy overly aggressive stocks, but they do rely heavily on earnings forecasts. This is a style that is usually devoid of extremes: not too much income and not too much risk. One might say that if all of the fund's assets were going to be placed with one manager, this style most likely would be selected.

An unfolding trend, which appears to be transparent to many investors is the growth of the convertible bond market. It has been very attractive to own high-yield securities that can be converted into equities. The one thing that inherently accompanies the ownership of convertible securities is the fact that most of the companies that issue convertible debt are the middle capitalization–size companies. They do this to reduce the yield on the bonds that they are issuing. They give a little bit of a supercharger effect to the debt securities so that they do not have to pay as much in interest.

INCOME GROWTH MANAGERS. The primary purpose in security selection is to achieve a current yield significantly higher than that of the S&P 500. The stability and rate of growth of the dividend are also of concern to an income buyer. These portfolios may own more utilities and fewer high-tech stocks and may also own convertible preferreds and convertible bonds.

Income growth is used primarily to fund higher-income needs such as endowments. The growth portion is the exposure to equities to provide an increased amount of cash flow and increase the value of the portfolio, perhaps to keep up with or stay ahead of inflation.

This type of manager falls into income growth but utilizes its own subasset category known as convertible bonds. The downside protection of a convertible bond portfolio is what makes it attractive. It is a way to take highly volatile stocks and reduce that volatility with the fixed-income component.

However, the performance of those types of securities in a market that was not necessarily favorable to medium- to small-cap stocks meant that the convertible bond manager was making a lot of the return from the income and not necessarily getting as much advantage from the equity side until that portion of the market turned around in the way the small-cap managers did.

INDUSTRY ROTATORS.   The primary emphasis of industry rotators is on finding industries that will outperform the market as a whole. They begin with a top-down approach that requires them to make projections and forecasts about general economic conditions. This "macro" approach leads them to over- or underweight certain industries that are consistent with their economic scenario.

An industry rotator is a manager who will identify specific industries that have moved because they are undervalued or have moved into a trend that the market is supporting highly. For example, in the early 1980s, oil stocks had been doing exceptionally well as an industry, and a rotator might have been very heavily involved in owning those stocks. As rotator managers moved farther into the 1980s, there was a heavy concentration in aerospace stocks and away from oil and gas stocks.

The managers can do a very good job if they have a lot of analytical expertise in the industries in which an investor is interested.

FIXED-INCOME MANAGERS.   Fixed-income managers use strictly cash-flow-generating instruments: bonds, notes, CDs, preferreds stocks, and the like. The advisors primarily try to maximize the highest yields while attempting to protect the principal by adjusting maturities to take advantage of rising and falling interest rates.

CASH MANAGEMENT MANAGERS.   Short-term fixed instruments make up these portfolios' liquidity, and maximizing principal protection is the primary objective. Even though these accounts have short-term (one-day) liquidity, they typically pay more like the 90- to 180-day CDs than like passbook or 1-week CDs.

Fixed-income and cash management are driven by the immediate need for the money. If the need for the money has a very short time horizon for liquidity, obviously that will be one of the major factors that drive the use of a fixed-income or cash manager.

9

E-TRADING

LARRY **CHAMBERS SAYS:** "On-line investors are looking at the wrong benefits. You may get the lowest price at the fastest speed, but is that really going to make a difference in your overall investment planning? The principles of investing will always hold true, and a clear understanding of how markets work is the only safe road to success."

Technology has given ordinary people complex investment tools without good advice on how to use them or evaluate their choices. For those who aspire to trade on-line, the amount of *mis*information is staggering. The factors involved—live quotes, execution routing and speed, live trade confirmation—as well as the variety of fees charged can greatly affect the profitability of the most astute trader.

Many deep-discount sites are simply taking orders from clients via E-mail instead of by phone. Then they route and execute those orders by using their standard paths. The additional services a site offers are generally proportionate to the higher fees they charge. A few sites actually allow traders to route their own orders in the networks and watch their live execution. However, the price for live trading demands frequent transactions and requires costly software.

As a result of having less interface with clients, a discount fee brokerage site can charge lower commissions. However, it may pass along additional costs (including ECN (Electronic Communication Network) fees and "postage and handling" expenses) to the client that previously were embedded in the commission charges. These costs can eat up any perceived savings.

The key is to gain an understanding of how trades are executed, what affects the cost of a trade, the limitations of one's own operating system, and how the Internet potentially aids or hinders profitable trading. Investors' trading habits, such as the frequency with which and the time of day when they are most likely to place orders, determine the extent and cost of services they require from a trading site or could obtain from other sources.

The hottest investment books on the market focus on day trading. It seems that everyone wants to get rich quick by picking the hot stocks and trading them on a daily or even hourly basis. As recent studies have proved, this is a surefire way to achieve frustration and chaos in your life. If you guess right once, you will guess *wrong* twice.

Are there success stories at E-trading? Absolutely, and there's always a lottery winner. The stock market is no more predictable than is a slot machine in Las Vegas. In my opinion, you have as much chance of successfully day-trading stocks as you do winning of the casino of your choice.

I personally trade on-line, but I am a buy-and-hold investor. That hasn't always been the case. I wanted to test my luck at day trading early in 1999, and so I moved $10,000 into a Schwab account. I read research reports, studied NAV graphs for trends, and then picked three local stocks that were trading at about half their record highs. I thought I could spot the low point and maximize my upside potential. Like many inexperienced day traders, I bought one stock at $2, sold it at $1, bought it back at $.63, and finally sold it at $.08. I then bought another stock at $10. It went up to $11.50, and then the company reported earnings of −$7.50 per share instead of Wall Street's estimate of 43 cents per share. Needless to say, my investment was cut in half before my sell order was processed. That lesson eventually cost me 85 percent of my investment. Unfortunately, many investors respond to similar experiences by investing more to recapture their losses. I will stick to the Churchill Downs racetrack for my "day-trade" money; the odds of winning are better.

Since E-trading is a hot topic for several publishers, I was able to gather a significant amount of information to guide you safely through the maze.

I asked my editor and author, Larry Chambers, to share his thoughts about E-trading from his latest book, *The Online Broker and Trading Directory*. Before becoming a financial industry trade writer, Larry was a national "top 10" broker with a major Wall Street firm.

Chambers believes the Internet is an excellent place to execute trades to save time and money but cautions that there is a huge distinction between electronic trading, day trading, and simply buying a security on the Internet.

Chambers says, "The number of on-line trading firms has increased from fewer than a dozen two years ago to close to 200 at the printing of this book. Trading sites fall into many different market segments, from so-called full service firms such as Charles Schwab and Waterhouse Securities, Inc., which also offer local branch offices and a full range of products, to firms such as E*Trade and Ameritrade and deep-discount sites such as Datek and SureTrade that exist only on-line.

"On-line companies like to boast about their phenomenal growth and try to overlook the fact that complaints continue to mount. Internet bulletin boards are awash with messages from on-line traders complaining about not being able to access their accounts, long delays in execution, and other major problems. Unwary on-line traders are being duped by stock tips planted on electronic bulletin boards, and other scams are sure to surface. Another complaint is that while some sites are promising that investors can buy initial public offerings, the truth is that only a few select on-line customers ever get a chance to invest in IPOs.

"There is a 'down-line' time gap through normal Internet channels, sometimes as much as 20 minutes. Thus, what appears on the monitor as a 'real-time' quote can vary greatly from the actual market price. Likewise, orders routed through this system suffer some delay before execution. Delayed confirmations can result in duplicate orders that are the trader's responsibility. Also, if you pay just an eighth of a point more than you intended because your trading site is slow to execute a 2000-share trade, the trade will cost you an additional $25. Most investors aren't even aware that they can lose that eighth of a point or how or where to go to avoid losing it.

"The on-line trading sites have no idea of your level of sophistication or lack thereof. The National Association of Securities Dealers, which regulates the brokerage industries, is considering new rules that would require on-line firms to determine the suitability of some investors for day trading."

Chambers's suggestion is to get as much information as you can before investing and never base an investment decision on what you read in a bulletin board. "The SEC has 100 lawyers who are spending a minimum of two hours a day surfing the Internet for illegal stock touting, and Internet fraud is becoming one of their top priorities."

Following is Chambers's basic description of the facets of on-line trading.

DIFFERENT TYPES OF INTERNET TRADING

On-line trading is simply investing by using the tools of the Internet. This can be short- to long-term investing; an investor may carry a position for a day to many years. The speed of execution is measured in minutes. You have access to all the markets on the Internet or dial-up or through proprietary software controlled by your brokerage firm.

The *first-time investor* (inexperienced) wants to make a trade without having to discuss it with his or her broker, may want a little more "hands-on" access to his or her investments, or may never have bought a stock from a broker, advisor, or financial planner, but wants to get started. The Internet provides easy, virtually anonymous entry into the trading world with little or no ongoing obligation. With the data and help screens available, an inexperienced investor can build and manage an entire portfolio or make just a single trade.

The *do-it-yourself investor* (experienced) is already using the Internet to enter orders, make switches, and improve stock positions. These people know how to navigate the research sites and take a quick look of the market. They typically make 25 trades a year, or 2 a month. That's still investing, not day trading.

On-line trading offers a major advantage to an *active investor* handling multiple transactions as well as the *financial advisor* of tomorrow. This person may be a full-service broker who has more foresight than his or her Wall Street cousins who believe that trading on the net is a fad. A recent study shows there are 40 million brokerage accounts but 15,000 new on-line accounts opening daily. That means 10 percent of New York Stock Exchange (NYSE) trading is done on-line. Almost every investment product is now available on-line, and performance analyses and portfolio management systems are updated electronically. Internet communication between clients and their financial services providers are immediate and constant, providing more accurate and comprehensive data to the client and freeing the financial advisor's time.

Then there is the aggressive *day trader* who is looking to capitalize on small movements of stocks on an intraday basis, ignoring the fundamentals of the underlying securities. The time frame for holding a security is usually minutes, with no overnight positions. Some of these investors trade up to 500 times a day. They generally are required to maintain a sizable account and pay substantial fees for their access to the actual market. This type of trading comes with high-risk warnings and should be engaged only in by those who fully understand the techniques. It is little wonder that these traders often make this their full-time occupation.

INFORMATION EXCHANGE: LEVELS OF DATA

Electronic day traders use real-time quotes and decision-support software that enable them to see market makers adjusting their quotes as the adjustments happen. The visual capability that comes from state-of-the-art software and technology that provides streaming quote screens, charts, real-time executions, and the last trade and volume executed has come a long way over the last few years, but not all sites offer these tools. Nasdaq provides several levels of quotes that disseminate varying degrees of information to the user.

A *level I* screen is what you'll find on most of the sites. Level I quotes display the inside market only: the highest bid and the lowest ask. For example, a typical level I quote might be INTC 128$^{1}/_{4}$ × 128$^{3}/_{8}$. This basic information is sufficient for most investors who make one or two trades in a month or a year, but a level I quote is fundamentally inadequate for gauging real market makers' interest in a stock. There is no way of knowing how much stock or which market maker is advertising to buy or sell. Because of normal market price fluctuations, a level I quote, as it appears on the screens, may or may not be accurate. A registered rep cannot guarantee a level I price to a customer.

For a subscription fee and with a possible upgrade of hardware, a *level II* screen shows not only the number of market makers but also the names of all the market makers and the amounts that they are advertising to buy or sell. This makes the screen an invaluable tool for gauging the strength and size of a stock and learning who the key players are. The real value of level II data is that it lets an investor choose an avenue of execution. The above quote on a level II screen might read INT 10 128$\frac{1}{4}$; GSCO × 1; 128$\frac{3}{8}$ MSCO 1; 128$\frac{3}{8}$ SALB 1; 128-3/8 MLCO 1; 128-3/8 PRUS. Until recently available only to professional trading desks and brokerage firms, level II is offered through several on-line trading sites and stock quote subscription services.

Level III adds an interactive element by allowing market makers to update and revise their quotes on any security in which they're making a market. The trader can observe and direct the actual execution of an order. Since this is a very costly service, it generally is used only by someone who makes frequent trades or engages in day trading.

CHOOSING THE RIGHT ORDER

Each of the following orders has its pros and cons, depending on the investor's situation, and considers current market conditions.

Market Order

A market order typically assures an execution but not a specific price. When an investor sends a market order, it will be filled at whatever price is available when the order reaches its destination. In a volatile market this can be substantially different from the price that was quoted.

Limit Order

A limit order is an order to buy or sell a stock with a price restriction. A buy limit sets the maximum price that investor is willing to pay, and a sell limit sets the minimum price at which the investor is willing to sell. It guarantees a specific price but does not guarantee an execution.

For example, an investor may wish to purchase a stock that is currently quoted at 15 bid, 15$\frac{1}{4}$ ask, but not want to pay more than $14. If that investor places a limit order at $14, it will be filled only if the price drops to 14 or lower and there are no orders ahead of that order. If the stock continues to trade at its current quote, the investor will not receive an execution.

Stop Order

A stop order is an order designed to protect a profit or guard against a loss. Although it does not work well in all conditions, it can be an effective strategy in certain situations. When placing a stop order, the investor specifies a price that when reached converts the order to a market order. For example, the investor may have purchased XZY stock at $40, and it is now trading at $60. If XZY drops to $50, the investor will want to sell the stock. The investor can place a sell stop order at $50, and if the stock trades there, the order becomes a market order to sell. The risk with this type of order is that once it is triggered, the order can be filled at any price because it is a market order.

Stop Limit Order

A stop limit order is a variation on the stop order. It works in a similar fashion in that it is triggered once the stock hits the stop price. However, instead of becoming a market order, it becomes a limit order at a price the investor selects.

For example, an investor wants to limit losses on a stock purchased at $50 and enters a sell stop limit order at "$40 Stop / $39 Limit." Once the stock trades at $40 or below, the order becomes a limit order to sell at $39. This will ensure that the investor will not sell at an extremely low price if a stock opens drastically lower. However, the investor still owns the stock since the order was not executed.

THE MARKETPLACE

The New York Stock Exchange

An individual cannot invest directly on the New York Stock Exchange. When one invests in person, over the phone, or on-line, one's broker electronically delivers the order to a specialist on the floor of the exchange. That specialist typically handles just a few stocks and is held accountable to ensure that his or her stock trades are fair and orderly.

ENTER AN ORDER through an on-line broker.

THE BROKER electronically sends the order to a "specialist" operating on the exchange floor or routes it to a floor broker at the exchange who physically walks the order over to trading area.

THE MARKET SPECIALIST consolidates the order with all others and then announces the best available price as well as the number of shares available at that price.

THE FLOOR BROKER makes a bid for the stock based on that price, competing with other brokers assembled in the trading area.

THE SPECIALIST awards the stock to successful bidders. If no buyers appear, the specialist is required by the NYSE to be the buyer of last resort. In exchange for providing liquidity in the stock, the specialist is allowed to profit from the price differential of the stocks he or she buys during price declines and then sells as the price rises.

The National Association of Security Dealers Automated Quotation (NASDAQ) System

Unlike the NYSE, this is not a physical exchange but instead a network of over 5000 broker/dealers who are connected through the *over-the-counter* (OTC) market. The OTC market is operated electronically via an open auction, without a central place or trading floor.

The Nasdaq market relies on these individual market makers rather than on a single specialist to provide liquidity in OTC securities. These market makers combine their efforts in each stock to provide a market collectively. This is referred to as honoring the two-sided market. Essentially, if a market maker is willing to sell a stock at one price, there must be a reasonable price at which he or she is willing to buy.

ENTER AN ORDER via an on-line broker.

THE BROKER transmits the order to (a) a single market maker (a Nasdaq-sanctioned trader who agrees to provide a market for the stock). The market maker fills the order from his or her own inventory, or (b) the broker routes the order through one of several electronic communications networks, where it can be seen by everyone with access to those networks. Competing market makers can then act on the order.

THE MARKET MAKER may sell the investor the stock at the ask price and then turn around and initiate a new lower bid to buy the stock back at a lower price. In this way the market maker profits from the spread between the bid price and the ask price.

The Middlemen

Both specialists and market makers create liquidity for every listed stock. In exchange for providing this liquidity, these middlemen are allowed to profit from the price difference (spread) that exists between the bid price and the ask price. Market makers and specialists are quick to raise a stock's price the moment they sense that a large institutional buy order is in the works or, conversely, lower the price when an institution attempts to unload a stock. To outwit market makers, funds and institutions break up large buy or sell offers and route them through an elaborate network of brokers, who in turn execute them over a period of days.

What would happen if these middlemen weren't on the job? The SEC pushed for the creation of the market maker system as a way to protect small investors. In October 1987, before the Nasdaq had its market maker system in place, share prices plummeted and institutional traders were able to negotiate direct sales. Individual investors, especially those holding small- and mid-cap stocks, had no direct access and were unable to find buyers. That of course caused their shares to plummet further. After that time, the NASDAQ *Small Order Execution System* (SOES) was created and made mandatory.

SOES gives small investors quick access to the Nasdaq market and enables the average person to get an immediate, legitimate execution and to bid and offer shares in between the spread to achieve price improvement. All these factors have an effect on what is sometimes referred to as market impact costs (also called price impact costs) and are the result of a bid/ask spread and a dealer's price concession.

THE FUTURE OF ELECTRONIC TRADING

A *digital stock market* (DSM) has received permission from the SEC to operate as an after-hours market, although 24-hour trading may be in the cards. The DSM will allow direct negotiating between on-line investors, bypassing the specialists and market makers, outside normal market hours. This means the actual buyer and seller will be representing themselves rather than working anonymously through an intermediary. The new direct trading system will provide sophisticated artificial intelligence software to match buyers and sellers.

The DSM evolved from a software program called the Chicago Match, which was tested for eight months on the Chicago Stock Exchange. The system works like this: You log in via your on-line broker, scan your portfolio, and select a stock. The first thing you see are orders broken down by size and price level, similar to level II quotes. After another mouse click you see the complete order book displayed on the screen, that is, the bid and ask prices from everyone with a current interest in the stock. You choose a buyer whose price you like and then enter into negotiations. You send a formatted message with a time limit to the other market participant to trade at a different price or a different quantity for your counterpart to accept, modify, or reject.

Currently, People's Stock Network buyers and sellers can trade 19 issues without the aid of a broker. Meanwhile, across the Atlantic, the Norex exchange, created by the planned merger of several Scandinavian stock markets, aims to be the dominant equity-trading forum in Europe, one that could give traders everywhere access directly via the Internet.

The Paris Bourse and the NYSE have opened talks about a possible linking that might also include exchanges in Canada and Latin America. The Nasdaq has completed a merger with the American Stock Exchange. The Chicago Board Options Exchange, which recently merged with the Pacific Exchange, will offer on-screen trading via OptiMark.

This trading system claims it will eliminate the need for market makers and specialists while providing sufficient liquidity. How? By lumping everyone's order together. You want to sell 100 shares of Disney? Your order gets aggregated along with Fidelity's 100,000-share purchase order and Merrill's and Templeton's, and so on. Theoretically, even the most seasoned traders won't be able to guess whom they're buying from.

Of course, it's not quite that simple. Remember how institutions break up their orders into little pieces that are traded at varying prices? An algorithm will let them do the same thing. Before they even enter the market, traders fill out an anonymous profile stating the exact number of shares a trader is willing to buy or sell at a cascading series of prices. The algorithm scans your profile along with the thousands of other profiles in the system and executes the trade, pocketing a tiny per-share commission. A computerized matching system will arrive at prices faster than traders can by using phones or even computer terminals. The prices will be more indicative of the stock's actual worth.

Can electronic matching systems outwit carbon-based traders and their gut-based strategies? Institutional traders are going to continue believing that they can beat the system, especially the people on the trading floor whose job it is to work the orders. Their value is that they sit there and decide how to break up an order and feed it out into the market. But instead of shooting from the hip during chaotic trading hours, traders now can map out these complex strategies in advance, the way a football coach designs key plays. Because of system security, no one but the traders themselves will ever see the playbook.

WARNING!

Unprecedented price and volume volatility have added another layer of potential problems that could affect order outcomes. Investors need to be knowledgeable about what volatility can mean in terms of additional risk and what one can do to limit that risk.

Extreme price fluctuations may give investors an unwelcome surprise when they place orders without real-time quote information. However, in a volatile market, quotes can be delayed by the source and therefore are not reflective of the actual market. In addition, under such conditions, orders are not always executed instantaneously. The result is an execution that can be substantially different from the price that the investor saw quoted.

High volumes of trading at market openings and at other points during the day may result in delays, causing orders to be executed at undesired prices. For example, many market makers will execute orders manually or reduce their size guarantees during periods of volatility, creating the potential for delays in order executions and losses.

As was mentioned earlier, market orders, by definition, must be executed by a brokerage firm as fast as possible without regard to price. For IPOs and under other unusual market conditions, it is possible for a market order to be executed at a price that is more than *100 percent* higher (or lower) than the indicated market price. Such price volatility may result in exceeding the buying power in an investor's account, in which case the investor will have only three days to deposit the additional funds required. With limit orders, although the investor is receiving price protection, there is always the risk that the order may not be executed. Limit orders are the default choice on most on-line order systems.

Wide price fluctuations and heavy trading are typical characteristics of "fast markets." These conditions and high volumes of Internet traffic can cause delays in the delivery of order confirmations. Before placing an order a second time, you should check your messages to see if you received a tracking number for your order. If you received a tracking number, you can be sure that your order is being processed; therefore, you do not need to place the order again. Any duplicate orders entered will be your responsibility, not that of the on-line brokers.

These conditions also can affect your ability to cancel orders. Under normal market conditions, you generally cannot cancel a market order. In fast market conditions, you may experience delays in canceling limit orders. When you attempt to cancel any order, especially a marketable order, during fast market conditions, your request is processed on a "best-efforts" basis.

As was suggested in Larry's remarks, be careful how you use this developing technology. Have fun with on-line trading but be sure not to rely on your stock selections for your retirement savings. With an investment option as risky as on-line trading, where it is easy to change holdings every minute of the day, you need to be disciplined. Start slow and, most important, know when to stop.

10

COMPANY STOCK OPTIONS

STOCK OWNERSHIP IS ONE OF THE TRADITIONAL WAYS in which the vast majority of U.S. corporations offer incentives to targeted groups of key employees. Among those methods, the ability to purchase company stock at a substantial discount (a stock option) is far and away the favorite. Although the employer must forgo realizing the profit on selling that stock on the market, an employee who is committed in the long term to work hard to increase shareholder value offsets that disadvantage. However, when these incentives are forgotten or overlooked, the performance-enhancing ability of these rewards is undermined. Most executives rarely devote time to planning how to maximize the benefits of their stock options.

This chapter will provide a detailed description of the different types of options and the benefits of each one. We will then hear from a stock option expert about how he perceives this corporate benefit and the potential pitfalls you could encounter by not carefully monitoring your options.

First, I'd like to share my personal experience with stock options. In the early years of my career I received only one form of compensation—cash. Later, when I joined Providian, I was rewarded with stock options with a three-year step-vesting schedule. However, in 1997 Providian was purchased by AEGON, and all my options were immediately vested.

Since I was making some improvements to my home, I decided to sell some of those options. This generated about $50,000, but after paying ordinary income tax, I netted only about $30,000. But that's not the bad news. If I hadn't exercised those options at that time, they would have been worth approximately $300,000 just two years later. Talk about hindsight. ... Although this was disappointing, my remaining options have increased substantially, and that has created another problem: Nearly 70 percent of my investment portfolio is in one company. Diversifying isn't easy since it could create huge ordinary income tax consequences. These are real problems investors face every day.

Fortunately, I was able to get Jeff J. Saccacio, partner in charge of the West Coast Personal Financial Services Practice for PricewaterhouseCoopers L.L.P., to explain how to maximize stock option compensation and avoid the common pitfalls. Jeff specializes in planning for high-net-worth individuals, entrepreneurs, and closely held businesses and has extensive estate- and trust-planning experience.

TYPES OF STOCK OPTIONS

After receiving stock options as part of his or her compensation, an executive needs to understand all the terms and provisions of the type of options granted. There are two types of stock options: *incentive stock options* and *nonqualified stock options*. Each carries very different tax consequences for the employer and the executive.

Incentive Stock Options

An incentive stock option (ISO) is a right granted by a company (the *issuer*) to an employee (the *holder*) to purchase one or more shares of the company's stock at a predetermined purchase price. Continued appreciation of the company stock after the grant date allows holders of the ISO to obtain the stock at a substantial discount. Depending on its terms, an ISO may be exercisable at the date of grant or over a specified period of time.

The issuer may grant ISOs to *employees* only and for a term of no more than 10 years from the adoption of the stock option. Also, no more than $100,000 worth of stock (valued at the time of grant) may be exercisable for the first time in any one year and at an exercise price not less than the fair market value of the stock at the time of the grant. The option must be exercised during employment or within three months after the termination of employment.

No immediate tax consequence results from the *grant*, or *exercise*, of an ISO. Also, the issuer does not receive the tax benefit of a compensation deduction for the difference between the exercise price paid by the employee and the fair market value of the stock on the date when the employee exercises the option to purchase the stock.

The employee will be taxed upon selling the stock, giving the employee control over the timing of his or her tax liability. The Internal Revenue Code provides favorable income tax consequences for option holders, taxing the income at capital gains rates if certain conditions have been met. Currently, the top federal tax rate on long-term capital gains (stock held longer than 18 months) is 20 percent and that for middle-term capital gains (stock held longer than 12 months but not for more than 18 months) is 28 percent. This is in contrast to the top rate of 39.6 percent for ordinary income. To qualify, the employee must hold the stock for at least two years from the date the ISO is granted and for at least one year from the date when the option was exercised (this is referred to as the *2 Year/1 Year Rule*). If the employee sells the stock before that time, the gain on the stock sale is taxed as ordinary income in the year of sale (essentially converting the ISO to a nonqualified stock option).

For example, a company grants an executive an ISO for the purchase of company stock with an exercise price of $10 a share. At some point in the future, when the stock has appreciated and is worth $50 a share, the executive exercises the options. In this case, there is an immediate increase of $40 per share in wealth to the employee, the difference between what is paid for the stock and the current fair market value, called the *spread*. The $40 spread is not subject to income tax, and the employee now owns the stock. That original spread, plus any future appreciation, is taxed only when the employee sells the stock. If the executive meets the requirements of the 2 Year/1 Year Rule, he or she receives a 12 percent to 20 percent tax saving depending on the amount of time the stock was held before its sale.

Nonqualified Stock Options

A nonqualified stock option (NQSO) is more flexible than an ISO. There are no limits on the amount of stock that can be exercised, the exercise price, or the term of exercise. NQSOs may be granted to an employee, independent contractor, or director. As with an ISO, any appreciation of the stock after the grant date allows the holder to obtain the stock at a discount. Depending on the terms, the options may be exercisable at the date of grant or over a specified period of time.

Unlike the case with an ISO, the recipient must recognize the spread as income at the time the NQSO is exercised, and the income is then taxed at ordinary federal income tax rates. This difference between capital gains and ordinary income tax rates is a major disadvantage, as is the fact that the recipient has not actually received any cash with which to pay the income taxes. Still, the recipient controls when the income is recognized by determining when to exercise the options. The issuer receives the tax benefit of a compensation tax deduction for the spread in the year in which the recipient exercises the option. Any gain or loss that occurs when the stock is ultimately sold is treated simply as a capital gain or loss.

Building on the prior example, let's say an executive receives an NQSO with an exercise price of $10. If he or she exercises the option when the stock is worth $50, the $40 spread becomes part of his or her income for that year's taxes. Not only is the spread taxable before the stock is sold, it's considered compensation, just like salary. Instead of being taxed at the preferential capital gain rates (as low as 20 percent), the spread is subject to a tax rate as high as 39.6 percent. Assuming the executive sells the stock 18 months later at a price of $60, that $10 increase in value will be treated as a capital gain and taxed at 20 percent.

In terms of managing tax liability and accumulating wealth with as little drag from income tax as possible, an ISO is ideal. However, if the holder of an ISO violates the 2 Year/1 Year Rule, the spread is immediately taxable as ordinary income. In essence, the ISO is converted to a NQSO.

ADDITIONAL TAX CONSEQUENCES

The Alternative Minimum Tax

There is one additional tax drawback: the alternative minimum tax. Individuals take advantage of certain tax benefits vis-à-vis deductions and the ability to exclude certain income from immediate taxation—such as the spread on an ISO—in computing tax the regular way. The IRS uses the alternative minimum tax to ensure that taxpayers don't "overuse" these benefits.

The government requires individuals to compute their regular and alternative minimum tax each year. In computing the alternative minimum tax, certain tax benefits are denied: Deductions are disallowed, and excluded income (such as the spread on an ISO) becomes taxable. To the extent that a taxpayer's alternative minimum tax is higher than the regular tax, the taxpayer must pay that additional amount. Depending on an executive's tax situation, the normally nontaxable ISO spread may unexpectedly become taxable.

Projections of regular and alternative minimum tax are necessary to determine the optimal time for an option exercise. These tax calculations should be performed over the planning horizon (the period over which the stock can be acquired) rather than for a single year.

This allows "what if" scenarios to be explored, ensuring overall min-imization of taxes and maximization of acquired wealth.

VESTING: HOW EMPLOYEES BECOME ENTITLED TO EXERCISE OPTIONS

Since employers generally grant options as an incentive, options rarely can be exercised immediately. Typically, options must *vest*. This means that the employee earns the right to exercise the options. Vesting can occur over a period of time or upon the occurrence of an event. For example, a grant of 5000 stock options with a five-year vesting period would mean that the holder would earn the right to exercise those options at the rate of 20 percent each year. In other words, at the end of year 1, the holder would be able to exercise 1000 options; at the end of year 2, 2000 options; and so forth.

LOSING OPTION RIGHTS: EXPIRATION, DEATH, OR SEPARATION FROM SERVICE

Expiration Period

When a company offers an option to buy stock, the option is gener-ally open only for a specified period of time. The *expiration period* differs from a *vesting period* because it is the date beyond which the holder cannot exercise options even if they are vested. If the holder is not actively planning to exercise the option, he or she may unknow-ingly let the option lapse and lose valuable compensation. Also, the holder may get boxed into a corner where he or she must exercise options or face losing some or all of them. The impact on cash flow and the associated tax consequences can be magnified in such an event.

For instance, on December 10, 1997, an employee is granted 5000 options that vest over a 5-year period, but the expiration date is 10 years from the granting, December 10, 2007. Assume that the employee remains with the company for five years and has the right to exercise all 5000 options but decides for whatever reason not to exercise them. If the employee doesn't remember that the right to exercise those options expires on December 10, 2007, and that date passes, even though the options are fully vested, those options will expire. The employee will lose a potentially valuable right.

Survivor Implications

Most stock option holders do not consider what will happen to their options if they die before exercising them. Typically, the period of time in which to exercise a stock option is compressed after the holder dies. In estate planning, liquidity has to be provided to meet normal concerns such as paying taxes and the day-to-day expenses of supporting a family. Additional liquidity needs to be available for exercising stock options.

Postseparation Issues

An executive also needs to understand what happens to the options that are vested under the plan when he or she leaves the company. For example, the executive has options to purchase 5000 shares of stock, and they vest over a five-year period. The executive gets another job offer and decides to leave the company in year 3, vesting in 3000 of the 5000 stock options.

Many stock option plans say that if an employee leaves the company, the deadline to exercise the options comes sooner than it otherwise would have. It's conceivable that the expiration date could be something much sooner, even six months or a year after the employee leaves the company.

In addition, understanding the vesting schedule is very important. Knowing how many options he or she would be abandoning could enable the holder to negotiate with a new employer for some sort of compensation for the value of the lost stock options.

KEY DATES: NEWS YOU CAN USE

All the key dates and provisions of stock options plans are crucial information for wealth accumulation and tax planning:

- Grant date: the date you are given the option to purchase stock
- Vesting date: the date you acquire the right to exercise options
- Exercise date: the date you exercise your right to acquire stock and pay the exercise price
- Exercise price: the predetermined price you pay to acquire stock
- Expiration date: the normal date after which you can no longer exercise options even if you're vested
- Postseparation expiration date: the expiration date after you are terminated or leave the company

At least once a year (at a minimum in conjunction with year-end tax planning) a holder should compare the exercise price to the fair market value of the stock he or she has the option to acquire. Preferably, this should be done every quarter. Keeping track of how much the company's stock is worth is essential to making the best decision about an appropriate time to exercise stock options. If the value of the stock is sufficiently above what the holder must pay for it, it may be an attractive time for the holder to exercise the options.

Another key component is an analysis of the tax consequences. A tax advisor can best analyze the tax impact of exercising the options. It may be more advantageous to the holder to exercise options over a period of time or to exercise them all at once. The object is to exercise options in the most cost-effective and tax-effective manner.

FUNDING THE EXERCISE: CASHLESS EXERCISE OR STOCK SWAPPING

Taxes are not the only cost of exercising stock options. An executive needs to understand the mechanics of paying the exercise price. This involves cash, borrowing, or more unusual concepts such as a cashless exercise or stock swapping.

Cashless Exercise

An executive can concurrently exercise the right to acquire stock and sell as many shares as necessary to pay for the exercise and the tax. That transaction is a cashless exercise.

For example, the exercise price for each share of a nonqualified stock option is $2 and an executive has 10 options. The fair market value of the stock is $5. It would cost the executive $20 to acquire all 10 shares; the shares would be worth $50. A cashless exercise would require selling 4 of the 10 shares to pay the exercise price. The holder would end up with 6 shares worth $30, excluding transaction costs and taxes.

Stock swapping

Another method of exercise is stock swapping. For example, if the holder owns 4 shares of a stock that is now worth $5 a share plus a stock option to acquire 10 more shares at $2, he or she can exchange the 4 shares of stock to exercise the 10 options. The holder will then own 10 shares worth a total of $50.

Swapping is *not* considered a taxable event. The IRS doesn't treat the above transaction as if the four shares were sold, but the executive does have to pay tax on the spread on the exercise of the nonqualified stock options.

Summary checklist

- Know the type of options granted and the key dates.
- Understand the tax consequences of stock options.
- Calculate tax liability under alternative scenarios before exercising options.
- Time the exercise of options to properly manage tax liability and cash flow.
- Examine financing alternatives and their respective consequences on cash flow and wealth accumulation planning.
- Know the effects of employment separation on key options' dates.
- Know the consequences to heirs if there are unexercised options at death.

WEALTH WITHOUT TAX

Part 3 will discuss certain types of investments that afford tax deferral or tax-free growth. We will not discuss life insurance as a means of accumulating wealth without paying tax since life insurance is not an investment product. I have included a description of the different types of life insurance in Appendix B. This is an important distinction. If you need life insurance, variable universal life (VUL) can provide a great combination of tax benefits and life insurance. Up to this point, it has been difficult for consumers to find a VUL that is cost-efficient.

I will address another type of insurance in this part: variable annuities. Annuities have very little death benefit cost since they typically provide only a guarantee that you will not pass less to your heirs than you contribute. This small amount of death protection and the associated cost do not outweigh the benefit of tax deferral for long-term investors.

11

TAX-EFFICIENT INVESTING

IN THIS CHAPTER we will limit the discussion to tax-efficient investing using securities products. As you may be aware, mutual funds typically are *not* known as tax-efficient instruments. Separate managed accounts and individual stocks are considered more tax-efficient than mutual funds, since a fund manager typically buys and sells stocks and passes the taxes on to the shareholders. If you purchase an individual stock, you pay tax on the gain only when you decide to sell the stock. Dividends from the stock are taxable each year, but you can get around this by purchasing smaller capitalization stocks that do not pay a dividend.

But what about the mutual fund world? Is there a way to pay less tax without the higher level of risk an investor assumes by purchasing small cap stocks? The answer is yes. It hasn't been that long since some fund company decided that they would manage their mutual funds with the objective of achieving growth with lower taxes. The strategy is quite simple. Near the end of the year the manager of the fund looks at the buys and sells over the course of the year and estimates how much capital gains will have to be distributed to the shareholders. The manager then looks for stocks in the fund that lost value and sells those stocks to offset the gains from previous sales. The result to the mutual fund buyer is a reduction in the amount of tax due for the long-term gains realized by the fund. The manager also tends to hold securities for at least one year to minimize short-term capital gains.

The shareholders of the fund have two risk issues to consider. The first is that the distribution of dividends cannot be deferred easily. If the manager attempts to reduce the dividends of the fund, he or she is probably purchasing stocks of companies that are smaller in size or may be unstable.

The second issue is the accumulation of unrealized gains of the fund. As the mutual fund manager sells losers to offset the gains incurred during normal trading throughout the year, the fund becomes very heavily weighted with winners.

Many tax-managed funds have 50 to 100 percent unrealized gains within the fund. The danger to a new investor in that fund is that the investor buys in today and the fund has a need to sell the winners without any remaining losers to offset the gain. In this case the investor could end up paying capital gains taxes on a distribution even if he or she has not achieved any growth.

Now let's hear from the top financial advisors on how they do tax-efficient investing and whether they use tax-efficient funds.

HOW DO YOU MANAGE MONEY TAX-EFFICIENTLY?

Ray Ferrara uses a private money manager and works closely with the manager and the client to offset losses, where possible, against gains. He also times sales so that any income tax or capital gain liability is spread out over more than one tax period. Regarding mutual funds, he uses tax-managed funds where appropriate.

Thomas Muldowney does what he calls *tax engineering*. For example, he uses bonds in the deferred and sheltered accounts and deferral in the capital gains accounts, using municipals and/or annuities when and where appropriate.

Kelley Schubert, who is also a practicing CPA, believes tax efficiency is of paramount importance: "One of the best ways to achieve tax efficiency is with an S&P 500 index fund or a marketwide index fund. These funds rarely recognize capital gains, and if they do, the gains are always long-term in nature. Additionally, one should use only mutual funds that strive to match gains and losses in a particular year so that the capital gain distributions are kept to a minimum."

John Bowen, Jr., points out two approaches toward tax efficiency that he uses for his clients:

1. Treat the client's portfolio as a whole by aggregating it; however, look at each area where a client is holding his or her positions. For example, to the extent that the client has fixed income in the portfolio, look to place that income in qualified accounts, such as individual retirement accounts (IRAs), to mitigate the current income.
2. Choose each asset class mutual fund for its tax efficiency. For example, large cap growth positions, such as a market portfolio, are inherently tax-efficient, whereas small and value positions aren't. In those types of asset classes in which they are not tax-efficient, choose mutual funds that are tax-efficient and realize short-term losses, hold positions to maintain capital gains, and invest to reduce dividend outflow. Also, make sure clients have positive cash flow coming in to help them with realizing tax losses.

Marilyn Bergen finds that clients all have different needs, but she tries to incorporate tax planning into portfolio strategies. Some of the ways she manages money tax-efficiently include the following:

- Use of index funds in large and small U.S. categories
- Use of municipal bonds and municipal bond funds
- Tax-loss harvesting when possible

■   Placement of higher-paying dividend investments within qualified
    plans, if possible, instead of in a taxable brokerage account

Kim Foss-Erickson integrates all tax-efficient investments,
including municipal bond funds, zero coupon bonds, and variable
and fixed annuities, as well as tax-managed mutual funds and qualified plans. "Every client situation is different and requires various
tax-planning tools."

Douglas Baker brings up a good point: "If we're talking about
outside a qualified or deferred arena, prudent portfolio management
and tax efficiency may be contrarian goals." It is his belief that while
earning a satisfactory return for the client is certainly important, the
primary reason he is hired is to keep the client from losing money.
He advises that advisors must be mindful of the "givens" in the
industry, such as not buying into a mutual fund just before gains are
distributed or purchasing shares in a fund known for its "quick
turnover." But if an investor is moving from a sliding sector or a well-
performing fund, there may be tax consequences. Douglas suggests
that the fact that a client may pay some money in taxes for money
made is far better than paying no taxes because of money lost. The
tax bite must play second fiddle to the preservation of capital.

Patrick Moran and Tom Nohr think the use of tax-managed
mutual funds, stocks, and variable products such as annuities is prudent.

Wayne Caldwell believes that first and foremost an advisor
should not let tax issues push him or her over the line to where he or
she is not doing the best job of financial planning or investment management for the client and, more important, cause the advisor to go in
a direction that on a personal level is uncomfortable for the client.
Wayne is very intent on incorporating tax-efficient strategies into
wealth management. "Too often in the financial services industry,"
he says, "I see very complex, highly regulated, and seemingly tax-
efficient strategies recommended to clients before the basics of tax-
efficient investing have been utilized. Incorporate as many of these
basic tax-efficient strategies as possible before looking at more elaborate tax-sensitive strategies."

What Are the Basic Strategies?

Wayne explains that in the current tax environment there is an overwhelming benefit for clients who do two things. First, you should convert wealth accumulation to the most tax-favored treatment, long-term capital gains, which you can control when you trigger the tax liabilities. Second, you should take full advantage of opportunities to put away money in before-tax dollars. This way, you're taking advantage of the two most tax beneficial approaches: one for tax-sensitive accounts and one for qualified retirement plans and IRAs.

In the taxable portfolio, one should create as many unrealized, long-term capital gains as possible. It is advisable to reduce taxable dividends and interest and reduce or eliminate realized short-term capital gains. An advisor should also manage the realization of long-term capital gains. One of the most basic approaches to this strategy is to reduce portfolio turnover dramatically. That alone adds significantly to the tax efficiency of any strategy.

It is best to look for asset classes that are inherently tax-efficient, buy them, and hold them for the long run. You should sell only when you need to take distributions or create cash flow from your portfolio. When you're looking for periodic cash flow or income, don't be concerned about the source of the income and allow that income to come from the most tax-efficient part of the portfolio. What that means is that you should not worry if you're not generating a lot of taxable dividends. As you take income, you can make sales, trigger the long-term capital gain, and take that income stream in a tax-favored manner. This is called a "total return distribution policy." It's very effective at creating cash flow tax-efficiently from an overall well-balanced portfolio.

An excellent example of a highly tax-efficient strategy is the use of the S&P 500. As an index fund, it inherently has low turnover. Occasionally, changes occur at the bottom end of the portfolio as companies move in and out of the S&P 500 index. Because this index represents the largest U.S. companies, rarely do they outgrow the portfolio and get sold. These are primarily growth companies, and this means the dividend yields are lower, adding to tax efficiency.

If you know you're not going to need cash flow, another tax-efficient strategy is to avoid reinvesting any of the taxable dividends or short- or long-term capital gains that are distributed from mutual funds. These distributions will have some unavoidable tax liability, but you can use them to avoid or reduce any additional tax liability that may occur if you make sales to increase cash distributions.

Let's take a look at some of the other asset classes that are necessary in the portfolio to create balance and full asset allocation but may not be as inherently tax-efficient as the S&P 500. These asset classes include U.S. large value, U.S. small growth, U.S. small value, and a number of international asset classes. In these asset classes, one should still follow the basics: Keep turnover to a minimum by using asset class or passive index funds. Move any taxable distributions and dividends from the portfolio to a cash account. Don't sell unless you need more cash flow than is covered by the funds. Controlling dividends is a little more difficult in a large-value asset class, because these stocks tend to pay higher dividends than do stocks in the S&P 500.

This is a good time to comment on taxable dividends and interest in general. If you're trying to be tax-efficient, you need to stay out of bonds or use tax-free bonds for your bond component. If you're going to substitute state tax–free municipal bonds for your short-term government bond portfolio, you need to be well aware of or work with an advisor who is very knowledgeable about the difference between them and government bonds. They're definitely not the same and do not have the same risk and return characteristics.

With a U.S. large value portfolio, we can add another level of tax efficiency by utilizing an institutional fund that is tax-managed. This means that fund turnover is kept low in the portfolio. When there is turnover, tax management calls for selling losers to offset gainers. Sales are made in stocks where there is a long-term gain rather than triggering a short-term gain. This minimizes the distribution of capital gains, and when there are distributions, they tend to be tax-favored long-term capital gains. If you take this tax-managed approach and add it to a long-term, stable, diversified portfolio in which you sell only when you need cash flow, the tax efficiency becomes very high.

This strategy works for foreign tax-managed mutual funds as well as small U.S. tax-managed mutual funds. One of the keys is that indexing, asset class investing, and passive investing are inherently much more efficient than active management with its higher turnover. It's critical to look to the basic strategies of tax efficiency before getting into more esoteric areas.

WHAT ARE YOUR THOUGHTS ABOUT TAX-EFFICIENT INVESTING, QUALIFIED PLANS, VARIABLE ANNUITIES, MUNICIPALS, IRAS, AND VUL PRODUCTS?

Lynn Hopewell believes that tax-efficient investing has more bearing on wealth growth than does almost any other factor. For example, better a fund with an average return and high tax efficiency than a fund with a higher return and low efficiency. Qualified plans and IRAs are almost always good if you can get them. Municipals have their place but often are selected inappropriately, particularly when the fixed-income portion of the portfolio is short-term. Variable annuities and VUL products have their place but unfortunately often are used inappropriately.

John Bowen, Jr., agrees that variable annuities can be very effective for clients who are making regular changes to their portfolios and/or have high-turnover managers but states that they are not as appropriate for today's passive type of investor.

John adds that municipal bonds are more appropriate from a peace-of-mind or behavioral viewpoint. His firm doesn't utilize them for its current portfolios because they are relatively short on their maturities at less than five years, and at that point the after-tax rate of return is roughly the same as that of government or high-quality corporate bonds. John suggests that an investor can also utilize a matrix pricing strategy, "riding the yield curve" to get additional rates of return that would not be available in municipals because of their significant bid-ask spread. His firm maximizes and utilizes IRAs effectively by allocating the fixed income of its clients. It is just beginning to look into variable universal life products, which can be extremely effective when combined with the estate-planning program.

Glenn Kautt recommends qualified plans or annuities, where appropriate, for clients with tax-qualified accounts from company or self-directed programs, including retirement plan rollovers, annuities, and other programs. Starting in 1998, he provided every client with a before-tax IRA with an individual analysis and recommendation for or against conversion to a Roth IRA. He continues to look annually at each client's situation in which a conversion is not appropriate or possible. He also provides sophisticated tax analyses and recommendations for clients with stock options.

Harold Evensky believes all products should be considered: "In order of priority, always take maximum advantage of qualified plans and IRAs, municipals when the tax equivalent is attractive, variable annuities (VAs) rarely, and VUL when there is a need for insurance."

Kelley Schubert uses annuities, municipals, and life insurance to achieve a tax-advantaged position in an investment portfolio after maxing out contributions to a qualified plan such as a 401(k) or profit-sharing plan.

Variable annuities and variable universal life offer tremendous advantages for many investors. Unfortunately, they are poorly understood, even by many financial professionals. We find many investors who own fixed or variable annuities that provide poor returns, yet they believe there is nothing they can do about that.

Ray Ferrara believes it is never wrong to take a gain, and quite often it is okay to reposition a loser (take the loss) to offset part of the gain: "The value of tax deferral is incredible. Although careful estate planning needs to be implemented (including wills, trusts, beneficiary designations, and charitable gifting) when a client has substantial assets in any tax-deferred vehicle (VAs, qualified plans, and so forth), the value of tax deferral often exceeds the income tax liability.

"Taking capital gains is a timing decision. You pay the capital gain either today or tomorrow. I know of only two tax-efficient ways to deal with capital gains, and neither is usually desirable. First, you can hold the investment until it goes back to its original purchase price or lower and avoid the capital gain. The second way is for the client to die, and with a step-up in basis, the heirs have no capital gains with which to deal. Taking a capital gain should be an economic decision, not a life-or-death decision."

Marilyn Bergen agrees that it is important to consider tax implications in making investment decisions and commonly recommends qualified plans, IRAs, Roth IRAs, and municipals to her clients. For clients who are employees, she normally recommends that they maximize their 401(k) [or 403(b), etc.] first and then fully fund an IRA. If they are self-employed or company owners, she suggests setting up a qualified plan that will allow them to make major tax-deductible contributions. These may include profit sharing, money purchase plans, simplified employee pension (SEP) IRAs, defined benefit plans, 401(k) plans, and occasionally simple IRAs.

For clients who have money in both taxable and tax-deferred accounts, Marilyn may recommend municipals for the fixed-income side of their portfolios. Occasionally, VAs make sense for a client, but she looks at the investment choices and the internal expenses. If the expense ratio is much higher than she would recommend and the VA is back-loaded, she waits until the back-end fees are gone or have declined to 1 percent and then does a tax-free exchange into a no-load, low-expense-ratio VA product. She doesn't use many VUL products at this time.

Wayne Caldwell says that "except for municipals, when you consider these investment options, you enter a very highly federally regulated area of investments. And many are also subject to various short-term and poorly thought out political tax changes that could retroactively penalize clients. Another problem is that they come with a certain amount of irrevocability. This dramatically reduces their flexibility through penalties or excess tax when changes may be contemplated. There are also potential income tax problems upon transfer at death."

Municipals certainly have a place in a high-net-worth client's portfolio. Unfortunately, they often are looked at in a very simplistic way and used in a portfolio without a full understanding of the risk and reward characteristics. A good example is that if you go long in the bond market (15 or 20-plus years) to obtain a relatively high tax-free return, you end up with significant price fluctuations as a result of interest rate changes. If you stay in short municipal bonds of high quality, such as AAA insured, the spreads in pricing from high-quality taxable government bonds is much less significant. If you buy a particular state's municipals for state tax benefits, that reduces your diversification and adds a level of risk, because you're holding state-specific bonds.

Finally, municipal bond trading is much less liquid than are stocks traded on major exchanges. The spreads between the buyer and the seller can be significant, and especially small amounts of a bond (less than $25,000 lot) can be expensive to buy and sell. Municipals have a place, but these issues must be understood.

Nonqualified VAs and variable universal life or whole life are investments that have significant tax benefits and regulatory issues. They're almost always funded in after-tax dollars. Variable annuities can be particularly problematic for high-net-worth individuals. Those individuals may have been in fixed annuities at one time and then were converted to variables. The bottom line is that their cost basis is very low and the taxable gain that has been deferred is very high. It's fortunate that these high-net-worth individuals usually don't need to draw out of these annuities, because that would create taxable income. They're really just using them as wealth accumulation tools.

However, when they learn that at the annuitant's death the VA (assuming it's not going to a surviving spouse) will be subject to estate and income tax at the beneficiary level, the strategy becomes much less desirable. When they learn that it's difficult, if not impossible, to transfer a deferred annuity to a charity while one is still alive without triggering income tax, they begin to understand the lack of inflexibility of this investment strategy. Finally, when they understand that at their death there will not be a step-up in basis as there will be in their growth assets, it's not uncommon for them to question the original advice that got them into this annuity. That step-up in basis allows the heirs to avoid any capital gains tax, and the date-of-death basis becomes the heirs' new basis. This doesn't happen with deferred annuities.

Variable universal and whole life investments have a different set of circumstances. The advantages over an annuity are that in later years the client can take income from the cash value without its being taxable. At death, the death benefit goes income tax–free to the heirs. What many people overlook is that the death benefit, if the policy is held in the name of the insured, is likely to be added into the estate and that Uncle Sam will take a piece of it as estate taxes. Establishing irrevocable life insurance trusts to hold life insurance so that the policy is transferred to the heirs before death eliminates the potential estate tax. When this strategy is used, death benefits can transfer state and federal income tax–free as well as estate tax–free.

Wayne Caldwell recommends the extensive use of qualified retirement plans and IRAs. With current tax brackets, high-income earners gain a significant benefit by funding their qualified retirement plans or IRAs to the fullest extent possible. It could be a company retirement account, a 401(k) plan, or even a $2,000 allocation to an IRA: "Any time you can make an investment and retrieve 25 to 50 percent of that investment amount from Uncle Sam to put into your retirement account, it is too good to pass up. The contribution of before-tax dollars outweighs any downside issues, such as penalties if money is withdrawn prematurely, the irrevocable nature of the contributions, lack of capital gains treatment, and the lack of a step-up in basis at death."

Douglas Baker has seen the industry go through cycles when one or more financial products became wrong for everyone or the best thing for everyone. Recent changes in tax laws have made variable annuities somewhat less attractive, and VUL policies are being abused and not fully explained: "Insurance is not and has never been an investment vehicle. Any investment activity within a contract is simply an addition to the reason for the policy: financial protection in the event of death."

Tom Nohr talks about rebalancing, which often triggers a tax: "Using variable products improves the net income. Personally, I like VUL because of its tax-free income potential. Qualified plans are probably the most used and the most dangerous if utilized to excess. For example, if you have a young married baby boomer, it is conceivable that a couple at age 65 could have $2 to $3 million between them. I never read about how to get the money out.

"To be successful, people must do a variety of things with different tax treatments. An absolute must is a Roth IRA if you qualify for the contribution. When you compare the 401(k) and the Roth IRA (the same size and earning the same rate of return) at retirement and when starting to take withdrawals, to net a thousand dollars for goods and services, the 401(k) requires a withdrawal of $1540 (assuming a 35 percent tax bracket) because of the taxes, whereas the Roth IRA requires a withdrawal of only $1000 because it is tax-free. Which account will last longer? The same applies to VUL. What happens if the tax rate goes up because there are more retirees than there were in the past? The investor could be in for a rude awakening."

As you have read, there is a consensus that taxes have to be managed. How they are managed and the products that are used to satisfy this need vary greatly. All the advisors agree that there is no single way to meet the need. Several concepts for reducing investment-related tax were introduced in this chapter. In the next couple of chapters we will look in depth more at a few, such as qualified plans, annuities, and municipal bonds. Appendix B outlines variable universal life, which is not an investment but a way to accumulate funds in a potentially tax-free environment.

12

QUALIFIED PLANS

IN THIS CHAPTER we will look at how investors can use quali-fied plans to achieve long-term wealth. For the members of generation X the use of plans such as 401(k), Keogh, IRA, and SEP is second nature. Gen-Xers have never known any other means of savings for retirement. The idea of a corpora-tion taking care of its employees during their working years and then paying them a steady stream of income when they retire is very for-eign to those between the ages of 18 and 33. Baby boomers, by con-trast, have had to adapt to the changing landscape of corporate-sponsored savings plans.

Most young investors are not inclined to believe that their employers or the government will provide for them in retirement. Therefore, investors between the ages of 18 and 33 are saving at a much higher rate per dollar earned than has any other generation.

Whether you are 21 or 55, qualified plans are a critical component in achieving wealth. Our experts are fairly consistent in stating that managing one's contributions is the foundation of a financial plan. They also agree that to reach their financial goals, investors have to develop a dependable income stream, control costs, and beat inflation.

They also say that the time to start is now. The age at which you begin does make a dramatic difference. If at age 25 you start putting $150 a month into a retirement account that's tax-deferred, by the time you're 65, you'll have $840,000. If you wait until you're 35 to start, you'll have only $300,000.

With tax deferral, your money will grow faster than it would grow at the same return rate without the tax deferral. Even after withdrawing all your money and paying current taxes, you most likely will still have more dollars than you would have by paying taxes as you go. The reason for this is that you are able to earn interest on dollars that normally would have gone to pay taxes.

A number of special plans have been designed to create retirement savings, and many of those plans allow employees to deposit money directly from their paychecks before taxes are taken out. Employers occasionally will match the amount (or a percentage of the amount) an employee has withheld from his or her paycheck. Some of these plans permit an employee to withdraw money early without a penalty in order to buy a home or pay for education. With those which do not allow early withdrawals without a penalty, sometimes employees can borrow money from the account or take out low-interest secured loans with their retirement savings as collateral. Rates of return vary on these vehicles, depending on what an employee invests in, since it is possible to invest in stocks, bonds, mutual funds, CDs, or any combination.

Let's get the opinions of our experts.

Marilyn Bergen says she has often worked with self-employed individuals who were using an IRA or a SEP IRA but were not taking full advantage of the tax-deductible opportunities available to them. By setting up a money purchase plan in conjunction with a

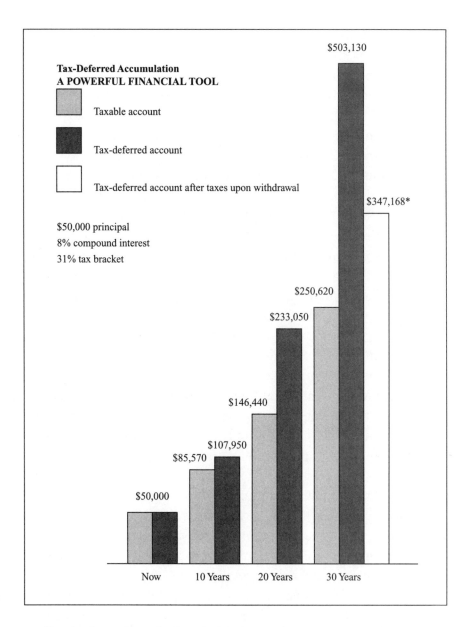

Tax-Deferred Accumulation
A POWERFUL FINANCIAL TOOL

Taxable account

Tax-deferred account

Tax-deferred account after taxes upon withdrawal

$50,000 principal
8% compound interest
31% tax bracket

$503,130
$347,168*
$250,620
$233,050
$146,440
$107,950
$85,570
$50,000

Now   10 Years   20 Years   30 Years

profit-sharing plan, she has helped people both save more in taxes and make larger contributions to their portfolios on an annual basis. Once they got into the habit of expecting to fully fund their qualified plans, many of her clients started setting aside even more money to build their wealth.

Marilyn feels, however, that there are several downsides to using qualified plans: "If the client is younger than $59\frac{1}{2}$, the money is normally tied up until he or she reaches that age due to the tax penalties. In addition, clients may end up with a disproportionate amount of their portfolios tied up in qualified plans and IRA rollovers. This can create complications for estate-planning purposes when a large amount of money is in an IRA."

According to Harold Evensky, all qualified plans have potential tax penalties and limited choices. In addition, I know Evensky would agree that the fact that many people still use only the fixed options within qualified plans is limiting the growth potential of those investors. Some providers of qualified plans are overcoming concern about these limited choices by changing the way they do business. A qualified plan provider in Purchase, New York, allows all participants to go outside the fund choices to Schwab and invest in any mutual fund or stock they like. This creates an overabundance of options that can be overwhelming for some. I do like the idea, though, since it eliminates the concern Harold expressed.

Interestingly, Glenn Kautt told us he believes that many advisors neglect to look at the long-term impact of specific distribution strategies in qualified plans. For example, selection of the method of calculating minimum distributions from a qualified plan can significantly affect the plan beneficiary. Once made, the calculation method is irreversible. Unfortunately, in many cases, little or no attention is given to this important issue, even by the client's tax accountant. The beneficiary may have to distribute plan assets rapidly, incurring a substantial tax. Where appropriate, we review the client's distribution situation carefully.

The downside of investing with taxes in mind is created by not looking at the entire picture. This is where comprehensive planning is the key and necessitates a program that takes into account the need for the distributions and the size of the plan assets. Other assets of the beneficiary can affect the impact of the decision on the distribution method.

Lynn Hopewell cautions, like Evensky, that the tax and administrative aspects of these investments can be complex and that extra time and attention have to be given to their correct interpretation and application.

With the downsides understood, any qualified investment advisor will recommend that you first contribute to your qualified plan, although there are potential tax penalties and sometimes limited options that create a need to invest outside the plan as a complement. Too many people rely on a 401(k) or Keogh as the fundamental savings option. This can be troublesome since at some time they may need access to additional cash. Accessing a qualified plan for that cash can create penalties and possibly keep the plan participant from contributing for up to a year. When you invest in a qualified plan, remember to also invest in something that is more liquid to help you meet the unpredictable demands of life.

13

ANNUITIES

A NNUITIES, PARTICULARLY VARIABLE ANNUITIES, have been largely misunderstood for years by investment advisors. I continually hear advisors, even some of the most respected, make blanket statements that these investment products have little, if any, value to a client. In my last book, *Guaranteed Income for Life* (McGraw-Hill, 1998), I explained in detail how variable annuities can be attractive as accumulation vehicles and are also the only product that can meet the goal of never outliving your income. We will discuss annuitization in detail later in Part IV on wealth protection, but since variable annuities are my personal specialty, I'll take this opportunity to discuss their features in detail.

All other investment products—mutual funds, stocks, bonds, and so on—share the same problem: Once investors begin to withdraw their funds during retirement, they run the risk of exhausting their savings before they die.

In general, there are two types of annuities: fixed and variable. The term *fixed* is used to describe the type of annuity referred to by the interest rate paid by the issuing insurance company. A fixed annuity offers security because the rate of return is certain. Typically, the insurance company promises to pay at a rate lower than the rate it expects to earn from its investment. The difference in rates sometimes is referred to as the "spread." It allows an insurance company to recover its administrative costs and profit. If for some reason the interest rate drops below the guaranteed rate, a bailout provision allows the contract holder to fully surrender the annuity contract and not incur any surrender charges under the contract. The name for this is a *bailout provision* or *escape clause.*

For example, a fixed annuity may offer a bailout clause for the contract to be surrendered if the current interest rate drops 1 percent below the interest rate in the previous period. Assuming that the prior interest rate was 6.5 percent, if the current rate for the next period falls below 5.5 percent, the annuity holder can surrender the annuity contract completely and not be subject to any contract surrender charges. The 10 percent penalty tax on premature withdrawals may still apply to a surrender under the bailout provision.

A fixed annuity also offers security in that the annuity holder does not take responsibility for making decisions about how the money should be invested. The amount of the benefit that will be paid out of the annuity when the contract is annuitized is also fixed and is therefore less risky, but it also may limit the upside potential. The settlement options the annuitant will receive from the insurance company will be the same each year during the annuitization phase. If the annuitant chooses a settlement option based on life expectancy, the same amount will come to that annuitant each month for the rest of his or her life without any investment decisions or risk on the annuitant's part.

For example, a customer has accumulated $50,000 in an annuity. He owns a 6 percent fixed annuity and wants to make consistent monthly payments over the next 15 years. He can plan on payments of $421 each month. At his retirement, his original $50,000 lump sum will have grown to approximately $76,000.

A variable annuity combines the best aspects of a traditional *fixed* annuity (tax deferral, insurance protection for beneficiaries, tax timing, controlled income options) with the benefits of traditional mutual fund portfolios (flexibility in selecting how to invest funds and the potential for higher investment returns). Variable annuities are often called "mutual funds with an insurance wrapper."

With a variable annuity, payouts are dependent on investment return, which is not guaranteed and fluctuates with market conditions. Variable annuities allow investors to direct their funds into several investment divisions, such as stocks, bonds, and money market funds. It is for this reason that a variable annuity is considered a security under federal law and therefore is subject to a greater degree of regulation. Anyone selling a variable annuity must have acquired securities licenses. Any potential buyer of a variable annuity must be provided with a prospectus, a detailed document that provides information on the annuity and the investment options.

Diverse investment options make it possible to structure an investment portfolio to meet a variety of needs, goals, and risk tolerances. These investments may be managed by a mutual fund company or by the insurance company. With the important advantage of tax-free rebalancing, investors can adjust their portfolios at any time. This allows an investor's advisor to carefully plan and manage the asset allocation strategy on the basis of changing needs or market conditions without having to worry about generating current tax.

Let's say you are a 35-year-old investing $10,000 in a low-cost tax-deferred variable annuity, and you're fortunate to get a return of 12 percent. By your 65th birthday you could accumulate over $240,000. If you are able to add $5000 a year all along the way, your $160,000 of total invested capital, compounding tax-free, could balloon to over $1,282,558. If you continue working and don't retire until age 70, your variable annuity could hold over $2,224,249.

Variable annuity investors also control their contract options. They dictate the amount, frequency, and regularity of their contributions; how their contributions are invested; and when the money is disbursed. The investor pays a premium to the insurance company which then buys *accumulation units,* which are similar to mutual fund shares, in an investment fund. The Internal Revenue Service (IRS) imposes no limits on the annual nonsheltered amount an individual may contribute to a variable annuity funded with after-tax dollars. In other words, you can put in as much money as you can afford. This is particularly important when it comes to supplementing retirement assets beyond the annual tax-free contribution limitation.

In both fixed and variable annuities, the investor does not have to pay income tax on the accumulated earnings until the payouts start. Unlike a mutual fund, an annuity does not pay out earnings or distribute any capital gains, and so these assets are compounded on a tax-deferred basis. The ability to reallocate assets without current tax ramifications, combined with the tax-deferred compounding of potential earnings, makes variable annuities a highly competitive investment vehicle.

When withdrawals do begin, taxes generally are paid only on the amounts withdrawn that represent a gain at ordinary tax rates, while the remainder of the account value can continue to grow tax-deferred. However, if the investor takes funds from the annuity before age 59$^{1}/_{2}$, there is an additional 10 percent IRS penalty on the withdrawal of any gain.

The amount of variable payments is not guaranteed or fixed and may fall in periods of market decline. However, if the annuitant dies during the accumulation phase (that is, before receiving payments from the annuity), the investor's designated beneficiary is guaranteed to receive the greater of the account's accumulated value or the full amount invested less any withdrawals and applicable premium taxes. Some annuities also offer "enhanced death benefits," such as options that enable a client to receive a step-up every six years until age 75 to lock in gains. Also, in most states this built-in benefit generally bypasses the delays and costs of probate.

Most annuities offer a free annual withdrawal provision that gives the investor access to up to 10 percent of the annuity's value yearly without paying surrender charges. Any distributions in excess of that 10 percent are subject to surrender charges.

Because of their insurance benefits, variable annuities generally cost more than do traditional taxable investments such as mutual funds. There may be front-end charges (although very rarely), management fees, and sometimes back-end surrender charges for early withdrawals from the policy. These charges and the length of time during which they apply to the policy vary widely across the industry.

Typically, a surrender charge is a percentage that decreases with each passing year, similar to vesting. For example, an annuity contract might provide the following surrender charges: year 1, surrender/withdrawal charges, 8 percent; year 2, 7 percent; year 3, 6 percent; year 4, 5 percent; year 5, 4 percent; year 6, 3 percent; year 7, 1 percent. Some have "rolling surrender charges," which means that each investment made has a new surrender charge schedule. In this case, if you invested $1000 every year, each $1000 contribution would have a new surrender charge schedule.

In addition to portfolio management fees, variable annuities charge a fee to cover the issuing insurance company's administrative costs and mortality and expense (M&E) charges. According to the 1997 Morningstar Benchmarks, annual M&E charges for the current industry average are around 1.3 percent and are increasing.

The higher the overall costs are, the longer it takes for the benefit of tax deferral to compensate for those costs. A no-sales-load, low-cost variable annuity can help shorten that break-even holding period. In general, variable annuities are designed to be held as long-term investment vehicles, and so a break-even period of 10 to 15 years may make variable annuities a good investment for investors with that type of time frame. Remember, the time horizon is not measured by when you will retire; it is measured according to the time when you would need to start withdrawals. Income distributions from a variable annuity are best used to supplement conventional retirement benefits or as a reserve until other payouts are exhausted.

Today's variable annuity managers, along with their affiliate mutual fund managers, seek diversification, consistent performance, and competitive returns by maximizing a portfolio's return and minimizing the level of risk. Variable annuity investments are often balanced by investing a percentage of assets in an annuity's fixed-income option to provide a less volatile investment return. These fixed annuity investments tend to smooth out extreme fluctuations. Investors won't profit as much from a good year in the market with such an annuity, but neither will they suffer as much loss of income during a bad year.

Deferred annuities, as we have been discussing, are the most popular form. They allow investors to accumulate money without paying current income tax on their earnings. This means that the amount can grow faster, because of the tremendous power of compound interest. Most deferred annuity contracts provide a greater amount of flexibility in the timing of premium payments and benefit payouts.

In contrast, an *immediate annuity* is one that begins paying benefits very quickly, usually within 30 days of the time it is purchased. By nature, it is almost always a *single-premium* purchase. An immediate annuity can be useful for an individual who has received a large sum of money and must count on these funds to pay expenses over a period of time.

For example, Mr. Jones sold his business. He received a lump-sum payment of $100,000 and purchased a single-premium annuity that would provide him with a monthly income. If he elected a settlement option based on his life expectancy, he could have an income that he could not outlive. If the sale of the business is Mr. Jones's only asset, he would not be wise to annuitize all of it. He would be better off annuitizing a portion and keeping enough liquid to meet unexpected daily demands. Annuitizations are powerful but can be dangerous for those without careful liquidity planning.

The single-premium option may be used to purchase either a fixed or a variable annuity, deferred or immediate. A single-premium annuity requires an initial lump-sum deposit (generally a minimum of $5000 to $25,000) and does not accept any future contributions.

For example, Bob Jones recently received a settlement from an insurance claim: a lump sum of $150,000. He does not need the money currently, and so he uses the funds to purchase a single-premium annuity for $150,000 and chooses to receive benefits at his retirement age by electing one of the income settlement options.

Other types of investors might be an athlete, actor, or artist who receives a large payment at one time and purchases a single-premium annuity that begins paying benefits when the person's career ends or a business owner who has recently sold his or her company.

A flexible-premium annuity allows payments to be made at varying intervals and in varying amounts. These annuities can accept future contributions and often require a smaller initial deposit. This type of annuity generally is used for accumulating a sum of money that will provide benefits at some point in the future. As with a single-premium annuity, a flexible-premium annuity can also purchase either a fixed or a variable annuity.

To recap, there are two phases of an annuity:

1. *The asset-building, or accumulation, phase.* A variable annuity is generally more appropriate for a customer with a longer time horizon to allow a substantial accumulation of wealth through equity investments on a tax-deferred basis. In the accumulation phase, the customer buys units similar to mutual fund shares. But unlike a mutual fund, the annuity does not pay out income or distribute any capital gains, and so the customer accumulates unit values over a period of years. These units also grow tax-deferred, making the compound effect even more dramatic.

2. *The payout, distribution, or benefit phase.* The payout phase begins when the insurance company starts making a series of payments consisting of principal and earnings for a defined period of time to the annuitant or the main beneficiary. Taxes are assessed only on the portion of each payment that comes from earned interest (except with qualified contracts).

There is no age at which distributions or benefit payments must begin for a nonqualified annuity, except in New York and Pennsylvania (age 85), which is not true for other types of investments, such as IRAs. However, most insurance companies specify the maximum age at which an annuity holder must begin to receive benefits paid out from the annuity. Like other annuity provisions, the maximum age varies in many contracts.

For some insurance companies, payments begin automatically when annuitants reach age 80 or 85 unless an annuitant declares that he or she does not wish to receive the income. Some annuities allow payments and benefits to be postponed past age 100. Other annuities, IRAs, and tax-sheltered annuities (TSAs) must begin making distributions of at least a minimum amount in the year after the year in which the individual reaches age $70\frac{1}{2}$. This is yet another benefit of an annuity funded with after-tax dollars: The investor is not forced into taking distributions that he or she does not want to receive.

When the time comes to receive the benefit payments from an annuity, the annuity holder must decide what portion of the payments he or she wishes to receive as a fixed annuity and what portion to receive as a variable annuity. Depending on the contract, some insurance companies will not allow an investor to retain funds inside the variable options during annuitization. The reason for this is that most insurance companies can't administer those funds, not because it's necessarily the best option.

Under the variable annuity payout, the annuity holder does not receive a check for the same amount each month. To understand this better, it is necessary to understand the concept of annuity units. An annuity unit is a unit of measure used to determine the value of each income payment made under the variable annuity option. How the value of one unit is calculated is a fairly complicated process involving certain assumptions about investment returns.

For example, Mrs. Carter, age 65, is entitled to a monthly benefit payment based on 100 annuity units each month. The amount of the payment will differ from month to month according to the investment results of the investment accounts or subaccounts. More specifically, if the dollar value of the annuity unit is $12 in the first month, Mrs. Carter's benefit payments will be equal to 12 times the 100 units, or $1200. The following month, if the units rise to $12.50, Mrs. Carter's payment will increase to $1250 (100 units × $12.50). In the following months, if the annuity value decreases to $11, Ms. Carter will receive a benefit check of $1100 (100 units × $11). Not all annuity holders are comfortable with this, and some like to split the difference between the fixed and variable approaches. The first payment of a variable annuitization typically is based on an assumed rate of 4 percent. If the subsequent payment checks received are higher than the initial check, you know you did better than an annualized 4 percent that month; if they are lower, you did worse.

The single exception to this is an immediate annuity, which does not actually pass through an accumulation phase but after it is purchased moves immediately into the annuitization phase.

Generally, there are four potential parties to an annuity contract: the owner, the annuitant, the beneficiary, and the issuing insurance company. The owner is the individual who purchases the annuity, and the annuitant is the individual whose life will be used to determine how payments under the contract will be made. The beneficiary is the individual or entity that will receive any death benefits, and the issuing insurance company is the organization that accepts the owner's premium and promises to pay the benefits spelled out in the contract.

The most common situation involves only three parties, since the owner and the annuitant usually are the same individual. Thus, the three parties are the owner/annuitant, the individual or beneficiary, and the insurance company.

Every annuity contract must have an owner. Usually the owner is a real person, but there's no requirement that the owner be a real person as there is with the annuitant. In most instances in which the owner and the annuitant are the same person, the owner pays money in the form of premiums into the annuity during the accumulation phase.

Also, the owner has the right to determine when the annuity contract will move from the accumulation phase into the payout or annuitization phase and begin making payments. Most annuity contracts do not specify a maximum age past which annuity payments cannot be deferred, but in most annuities, the age usually is well past retirement age.

According to the Internal Revenue Code, the annuitant is the individual whose life is of primary importance in affecting the timing and amount of payout under the contract. In other words, the annuitant's life is the measuring life.[1] The annuitant, unlike the owner and the beneficiary of the annuity contract, must be a real person.

The beneficiary has no rights under the annuity contract other than the right to receive payment of the death benefit. He or she cannot change the payment settlement options or alter the starting date of the benefit payments or make any withdrawals or partial surrenders against the contract. Under most annuity contracts, the owner has the right to change the beneficiary designation at any time. In a very general sense, the insurance company that issues the annuity contract promises to invest the owner's premium payments responsibly, credit interest to the funds placed in the annuity, pay the contract death benefit in the event of the death of the owner before annuitization of the contract, and make benefit payments according to the contract settlement options selected by the contract owner.

The Internal Revenue Code requires that all annuities contain certain provisions to be eligible for the tax benefits associated with the annuity contract, but there is considerable variation between companies. For example, all companies have a maximum age beyond which they will not issue an annuity contract. If an individual is 80 years old, he or she will not be able to purchase an annuity contract from a company whose maximum age is, say, 75. Financial planners should request a sample contract for each annuity product they work with to maximize their understanding of this issue.

The financial strength and investment philosophy of the issuing company should be examined. To evaluate the financial strength, one can look at the AM Best companies, Moody's, Standard & Poor's, or Duff and Phelps. The rating services examine the items connected with the insurance company that are important in gauging the effectiveness and probability of the company's performance in the future. They include a list of information evaluating the company's profitability and capitalization and its liquidity. In addition, rating services examine the company's investment strategy and marketing philosophy as well as its business practices and history.

[1]See Internal Revenue Code, Section 72-S6.

Here is a checklist of factors to examine:

1. Are there penalties for early withdrawals?
2. Are the withdrawal charges graduated over a period of years, or do they remain level?
3. How much can be withdrawn at any one time without a penalty?
4. If fixed, what is the current interest rate and how often does it change?
5. If fixed, what is the minimum interest rate guaranteed in the contract?
6. If fixed, is there a "bailout option" that permits the holder to cash in the annuity without incurring withdrawal penalties?
7. Are there front-end load charges or annual administrative fees? How much are they, and how will they affect the return?
8. If variable, what is the mortality and expense charge?
9. If variable, how many portfolio choices are there?
10. If variable, how many asset class portfolios are represented?

Only half of our panel members use annuities because of the type of clients they work with.

When one of Marilyn Bergen's clients inherits money, she recommends a variable annuity. This type of annuity can accomplish several objectives. All earnings will grow tax-deferred until they are withdrawn. In addition, the money is "out of sight" to the clients. They know they will pay tax penalties on any earnings withdrawn prior to age $59\frac{1}{2}$. For many clients who have a tendency to be spenders, a variable annuity can be an excellent way to set money aside for the long term and not consider it available for current expenses.

The conclusion I draw from this chapter is that annuities are a complex investment tool and need to be analyzed carefully after a few steps have been taken. A variable annuity is not an investment for short-term planning needs. Some annuity programs can be limited in their fund selection, and so it is a good idea to review several companies before selecting a program. Other downsides are weight costs, penalties, commissions, insurance expenses, fund selection, and what it costs to have these funds managed. One should ask the following questions:

1. Do you have sufficient cash liquidity to meet life-cycle demands?
2. Have you maximally funded your qualified plan?
3. Do you have enough investment liquidity to make large purchases such as a boat, car, or home or to fund a college education?

Make sure you work with an investment advisor who understands how variable annuities work and when they are appropriate.

14

MUNICIPAL BOND FUNDS

MUNICIPAL BOND FUNDS ARE ANOTHER MEANS of achieving higher after-tax returns. Investors can purchase a state-specific fund, a national fund, or an insured national fund. Each type provides different levels of tax benefits and risk. Let's examine the various types of municipal funds, the degree of tax efficiency versus risk that each one provides, and how using such financial instruments may provide investors with a greater net after tax (NAT) return than do many other types of securities.

WHAT ARE MUNICIPAL BONDS?

Very simply, mutual funds are investment instruments used to finance municipal governmental activities. They are not always guaranteed by the municipality, a common misperception.

Investors whose goal is simply to conserve capital and generate returns that keep up with inflation often look to municipal bonds with the idea that these bonds are fairly safe. Investors may believe this is the case because "muni" issuances often include language stating they are "backed by the full faith and credit" of the issuing authority. In addition to the safety that conservative investors think they are getting in municipal bonds, investors may believe that these bonds' tax-free status offers additional rewards. The combination of safety and tax-advantaged reward is irresistible to many who are not especially sophisticated about the securities markets and are trying simply to avoid making an investment mistake.

Municipals attract many wealthy investors for these reasons. These investors are not looking for growth; they've already made it. As an example, the largest part of Ross Perot's holdings is in municipal bonds. I'm sure if we asked him, he'd say he's not concerned about growth. But then again, who knows what Perot would say?

One drawback of municipal investments is that if rates fall and prices rise, you're not necessarily going to be able to take advantage of your good fortune because the municipalities may hurry to call the bonds away from you. Also, tax-free certainly does not mean risk-free: Remember the Orange County debacle of the early 1990s and the New York City difficulties of the 1970s.

Municipal bonds have high trading costs because there are large bid-ask spreads and significant market impact costs in the municipal marketplace. These additional costs eliminate the benefits of using an enhanced trading strategy such as the matrix pricing strategy we use in our government and corporate bond portfolios. The turnover required would simply be too costly. Because of their high trading costs, municipal bonds are suitable only for buy-and-hold investors who want to hold longer-maturity bonds or high-yield municipals.

A municipal bond *fund* is nothing more than a large grouping of various municipal bonds. These funds may be appropriate for someone in high federal (28 percent and up) and state (5 percent or higher) tax brackets. Most municipal bond funds invest in municipal bonds of similar maturity (the number of years before the borrower, in this case the municipality, must pay back the money to the lender).

The key advantage of a bond fund is management. Unlike individual issues, the fund managers can switch bonds from time to time within a fund. A bond fund is always replacing the bonds in its portfolio to maintain its average maturity objective.

WHAT ARE THE RISKS?

The main form of market risk for a bond is the risk of interest rates changing after a customer buys the bond; this is called *interest rate risk.* If market interest rates go up, the bond loses principal value; if market rates go down, the bond gains principal value. The longer the term of the bond is, the more the price will be affected by changes in interest rates. Whether the U.S. government, a corporation, or a municipality issues the bond, the risk is similar.

Bonds are also subject to *call risk,* the risk that the bond issuer will choose to redeem (call) the bond before the maturity date. The call provisions must be stated in the prospectus along with other special features, but a prospectus can be hard to understand.

A bond's current value is directly affected by changes in interest rates. The effect of higher interest rates on bonds is to lower their prices. Conversely, lower rates raise bond prices. The fluctuation is due to the fact that the price of a bond must offer a prospective purchaser current market rates.

There is a lot to understand before buying an individual bond. It is a somewhat different process from buying stocks or mutual funds, because only a certain dollar amount of each bond is issued and that amount is almost certainly much smaller than the amount of equity issued. Large companies have millions of shares of stock outstanding, and all shares of common stock are the same. To buy a bond, by comparison, the customer can't simply consult *The Wall Street Journal,* pick a particular bond, and place an order. Buying a bond means finding the owner (such as an institutional trading desk) of a bond that meets the investor's needs.

The owner of individual bonds has much greater control of both cash flow and tax consequences. The investor controls when to take profits and losses, basing that decision on what is in his or her best interest. If it matters to an investor whether a tax gain is taken in December or January, a bond allows that choice.

An individual investor with less than $50,000 to invest in bonds is probably better off in a bond fund or unit investment trust, receiving the advantages of diversification, professional management, and significant cost benefits. Any institutional investor buys bonds more cheaply than a single individual can, and the bonds in a mutual fund have been purchased at the institutional price. An institutional investor also pays a minuscule portion of the total price in transaction costs, whereas transaction costs can be significant for an individual, and it gets worse if the individual must pay for safekeeping the securities. A bond fund does, however, charge a management fee that might equal in yield the transaction cost an individual would pay.

A mutual fund pays dividends monthly since it owns bonds with so many different payment dates, whereas individual bonds pay out only semiannually.

The following is information an investor should consider before making a bond purchase:

- Security description: type of bond, purpose of bond, and issuer.
- Rating: for example, AA is better than A.
- Trade date: the date the bond is purchased in the market.
- Settlement date: the date the purchaser pays for the bond and interest starts accruing.
- Maturity date: the date the purchaser will be repaid the principal and the last interest payment.
- Interest payment dates: the dates interest payments are made, usually semiannually.
- Coupon: the fixed annual interest rate (interest income) stated on the bond.
- Price: the dollar price paid for the bond. (An offer price is the price at which an individual investor buys the bond; the bid price is the price at which an individual can sell the bond.)
- Current yield: the coupon divided by the price, giving a rough approximation of cash flow.

- Yield to maturity: a measure of total return on the bond at maturity.
- Par amount: the face amount of the bond when it was issued, normally $1000.
- Accrued interest: the amount of interest income (coupon income) earned from the date of the last coupon payment to the settlement date.
- Whether the bond uses a 360-day or 365-day basis to calculate interest payments.

The two major independent rating services are: Moody's and Standard & Poor's. Investment-grade ratings range from AAA to BBB– (Standard & Poor's) or Aaa to Baa3 (Moody's). Lower-rated bonds are considered speculative. The ratings are intended to help investors evaluate risk and set their own standards for investment.

Grades AAA through BBB are considered investment-grade, although many advisors confine their attention to bonds rated A or above. Ratings attempt to assess the probability that the issuing company will make timely payments of the interest and principal. Each rating service has slightly different evaluation methods.

To determine whether a municipal bond fund makes sense for you, compare your after-tax return to another type of bond fund. For example, if a municipal fund pays 5 percent versus 6 percent from a corporate bond fund, which fund works better for someone in the 28 percent tax bracket? Divide 5 percent by 0.72 (100 minus the 28 percent tax bracket). The answer—6.94—is your after-tax return. Therefore, the corporate fund needs to yield 6.94 percent to measure up.

Investment advisors utilize bond funds in different ways. Let's look at how a few advisors use the different types in clients' portfolios.

DO YOU USE BONDS? HOW DO YOU ANALYZE BONDS?

Harold Evensky is a proponent of municipal bonds but scrutinizes quality, name, characteristics (e.g., call provisions, premium/discount), and duration.

Kelley Schubert sometimes uses individual bonds as well as bond funds: "The purpose of bonds in my portfolios is to dampen the short-term risk that is inherent in equity investing. Since reducing risk is my primary purpose with bonds, I use only short-term maturities. Short-term bonds fluctuate less than long-term maturities as interest rates move up or down. There is also significant statistical data to suggest that the price fluctuations that come with long-term bond maturities do not generate higher rates of return. Therefore, long-term bonds appear to contain risks for which there is no compensation."

John Bowen, Jr.'s firm, like Schubert's, utilizes bond mutual funds for similar reasons: "In analyzing these funds, we recognize that the reason to incorporate fixed income into a portfolio is to mitigate the volatility of the equity portion of the portfolio. Given that, we want to have short to intermediate bonds, and we look to see that they are delivered cost-effectively. In addition, we look for funds that don't make interest rate bets but deliver market returns."

On occasion Marilyn Bergen uses bond funds in portfolios, but she normally ladders the portfolios with individual bonds. She typically buys only AA-rated or higher-quality bonds but occasionally purchases A-rated bonds if the maturity date is within two to three years. Her general rule of thumb is that if $500,000 or more is available to be invested in U.S. bonds in a client's portfolio, she'll consider individual bonds instead of bond mutual funds.

Interestingly, Stan Hargrave believes bonds are a *poor* asset for almost any need, including income. Foss-Erickson, Pelky, and Campisi all agree.

Ray Ferrara says that it ultimately depends on the client's risk tolerance level. When he does include bonds in a client's portfolio, he will often use mutual funds, UITs (Unit Investment Trust), or municipal bonds. He believes that bonds present short-term possibilities for capital gain but should be used mostly for income.

It seems that the top investment advisors agree that investment tax planning is critical to success, but how that planning occurs can vary. I am a believer in using different vehicles for different purposes. I utilize all the discussed topics in my own portfolio. I take full advantage of my 401(k) for long-term retirement savings and use variable annuities for additional long-term retirement savings, since

I am limited by top-heavy rules in contributing as much as I would like to my 401(k). I use municipal bond funds for more liquid-type savings. I also use variable life insurance for funding a college education, since the withdrawals can be tax-free.

The point I would stress here is that these tax-efficient vehicles are difficult to structure for the rookie investor. With any tax-favored investment, there are potential pitfalls. The government does not allow many tax "loopholes" for a reason, and when an investment is deemed tax-favored, a list of penalties for inappropriate use comes along with the investment. Many of you reading this book are do-it-yourselfers. When it comes to investment tax planning, I recommend seeking the help of a qualified financial advisor.

15

SPIDERS, DIAMONDS, AND OTHER ETFS

ARE YOU WONDERING WHAT SPIDERS HAVE TO DO WITH TAX-EFFICIENT INVESTING? The fact that large numbers of Americans have started investing in spiders and diamonds might seem odd to the rest of the world. The fact that some put their money in qubes and WEBs is even more mysterious.

These exotic-sounding products belong to a class of investments known as exchange-traded funds (ETFs), or simply "i-shares," since they give investors immediate access to a stock market index. Thus, spiders (Standard & Poors Depositary Receipts) are shares that represent the S&P 500 index; diamonds, the Dow Jones Industrial Average (ticker symbol DIA); qubes, the Nasdaq 100 (QQQ); and WEBs, any of a range of "World Equity Benchmarks" related to different stock market indexes and averages.

While some of these products, such as spiders, have been around for years, it is only recently that interest in them has soared. Spiders are now the most frequently traded shares on the American Stock Exchange. Barclays Global Investors, the world's largest institutional money manager, has already spun 30 of its WEBs. So popular have ETFs become that Barclays plans in the next few months to launch 51 more in America, and it is now having talks with the London Stock Exchange about launching the first European versions later this year. The Frankfurt stock exchange is understood to entertain similar ideas.

What makes ETFs such an appealing way of investing in an index is that they are neither mutual funds nor investment trusts. To the uninitiated this might seem a mind-numbing technical distinction, but it means that ETFs in effect eliminate the main drawbacks of the two most common vehicles for "passive" index investing.

Mutual funds are "open-ended" vehicles, meaning that every time an investor puts money in, the fund issues him or her new shares, and every time the investor takes money out, the fund redeems some shares. This has two drawbacks: A fund's net asset value is quoted—and thus investors can buy or sell—only once a day, and even investors who do no selling may incur capital gains taxes if redemptions force the fund manager to sell some shares.

"Closed-end" funds pose other problems. Like other corporate entities, they issue a fixed number of shares, which investors can then trade on an exchange. Pricing and trading thus are continuous throughout the day, but there is a catch: Temporary mismatches in the supply and demand of the shares can result in hefty premiums or, more usually, discounts to the trust's net asset value.

Enter ETFs. Because they are shares traded on a secondary market, dealing is continuous. Like other shares, but unlike mutual funds, they can be bought on margin (i.e., for an initial down payment) or sold short (i.e., borrowed and sold in the hope that the price will fall), which allows much more sophisticated trading strategies.

At the same time, ETFs retain some features of open-ended funds. Market makers can, for instance, settle trades by using the underlying shares rather than cash. In theory, this should prevent discounts or premiums to the fund's net asset value. It also cuts down on taxable capital gains.

Admittedly, the details are awfully complicated. Still, in America more and more investors are deciding that ETFs are a flexible and tax-efficient way of investing, even without understanding them entirely.

The tax efficiency of these vehicles is created by the ability to completely control the distribution of the gains. As with a stock, you realize the gains only when you sell. You have no manager to worry about.

4

WEALTH PROTECTION AND PRESERVATION

In this part, we will discuss the ways in which you can protect the wealth you have created. Improper planning and assuming greater risk than is advisable can result in enormous losses. The goal in this part is to provide you with a few helpful ideas that can help protect you while you are living and protect your heirs after your death.

16

ASSET
PROTECTION

APERSON CAN SPEND YEARS BUILDING A PORTFOLIO, and it can be taken away in a minute. I'm not referring to investment risk now but rather to wealth protection. In addition to getting the best advice on how to safely accumulate and grow a tax-efficient portfolio, a little time and consideration given to how assets are titled and how to minimize their exposure to liability is an equally valuable facet of financial planning, as we will soon learn from John A. Meier Esq.

John, the general counsel for Financial Advisory Service, Inc., in Overland Park, Kansas, is adamant regarding asset protection planning: "The United States has more lawyers per capita than anywhere in the world. We're one of the few English-speaking jurisdictions that allow contingency fees. Contingency fees are in lieu of paying a lawyer's hourly fees. Instead, if the lawyer thinks your case has merit, he or she can agree to prosecute the case on your behalf in exchange for out-of-pocket expenses and a substantial percentage of any settlement or recovery.

"This in effect enables the little person to go after the big company that has far greater legal resources. On the negative side, because it's difficult to prove malicious prosecution, this encourages litigation: 'I can make you spend a lot on legal defense just because I decide to sue you.' Most people don't realize how susceptible they are to legal prosecution. If you are a person with high exposure, which today is almost anyone with a high income or high net worth, you need to establish as much space as possible between your personal assets and the possible trouble. Hence, financial planning."

LEGAL STEPS TO PROTECT PERSONAL ASSETS

John explains: "There are some basic tenets of asset protection that are fundamental things that everyone should do and that don't necessarily require the assistance of an attorney."

Limit Your Exposure

If you are a consultant or have your own business, incorporate or create a limited liability company (LLC), which most jurisdictions now allow as a one-person entity. If your state does not allow this, you might investigate the laws in Delaware or somewhere else where you can register. In addition, it requires only a Schedule C to your federal 1040 tax return. You don't have all the corporate formalities you would have as a one-person corporation. A number of major accounting firms and law firms have switched to the LLPS, which is the professional hybrid version of the LLC.

Precautionary Steps to Take When Hiring an Advisor or Buying an Investment

Financial advisors, planners, and stockbrokers all have what is called an ADV. By law, they are required to give you Part II, which discloses fees and credentials, but you also should request Part I, which contains information regarding any disciplinary action against a broker. If the broker doesn't want to give it to you, it could mean he or she is hiding something. The SEC and the National Association of Securities Dealers (NASD) provide information on-line about all the investment advisors, stockbrokers, and brokerage firms, and you can phone your state's securities office and ask for information about any claims or actions against a specific advisor or broker. An explanation may be satisfactory, but you haven't done your due diligence if you haven't asked.

The basic caveat is, If it sounds too good to be true, it probably isn't true. If somebody is promising you ridiculous returns and you're interested, have your CPA and attorney check it out before you take any action.

Never Give Anyone a Power of Attorney

Never give a broker or advisor anything more than a *limited* power of attorney, which is simply trading authority. That's commonplace and the way an investment advisor works. Never, ever give anyone in this situation a general power of attorney. A general power of attorney over your assets creates 100 percent exposure and is appropriate to grant only to your spouse, child, or executor in case you become disabled and can't act on your own.

Insurance on Accounts

Most accounts with big brokers are insured up to $100 million with SIPCO insurance, and many brokerage firms also carry a separate policy with a major insurer. Like the Federal Deposit Insurance Corporation (FDIC) insurance that banks have, this insures you not against investment loss but against mistakes and criminal acts.

Personal Umbrella Insurance

Secure a good personal umbrella policy that will pay legal defense costs as well as provide coverage for settlements. Many times, the plaintiffs and the plaintiffs' attorneys won't seek assets beyond the policy. Otherwise, you're at a disadvantage when the plaintiff's attorney is working on a contingency fee and you must pay by the hour for an attorney to defend you.

Get an Annual Checkup

Just as you get a physical every year, you should have a financial portfolio examination as well. Beyond adjustments to ensure success in achieving your financial goals, there are all kinds of reasons to review how your assets are titled and, in doing so, to be conscious of asset protection concepts of estate planning. Find out where your accounts are custodial and how they are titled.

Identify Your Exempt Assets

Next, look at your *exempt* and *nonexempt* assets. The definition, as well as the value, of assets that are exempt from creditors varies from state to state. Become familiar with the exemptions that are available in your state and transfer the title of your nonexempt assets to a neutral entity. For example, a professional person with a securities account and malpractice insurance could hold title to exempt assets under state law, such as a house and a retirement plan, but should put nonexempt assets in his or her spouse's name. This would extend even to bankruptcy filings.

Basically, there are federal *and* state bankruptcy exemptions, and each state can in effect say which one it wants to apply. Under the federal tax law, if you file for bankruptcy, you automatically have an exemption from cancelation of debt (COD) income. Most state laws piggyback the federal laws. Also, the tax code in the same section gives you an insolvency exemption. In other words, you may not have to file for bankruptcy. If you file the right supporting documents to prove to the IRS that you're insolvent, you don't have to count your exempt assets in determining whether you meet the test.

RETIREMENT PLANS. An Employee Retirement Income Security Act (ERISA)-type plan is exempt from creditors. Although regular and Roth IRAs are not actually ERISA plans, most states have, by statute, exempted those plans from claims by creditors. We tell clients to be sure their state is protecting Roth IRAs from creditors before they convert. While the tax-planning aspects are important, it is not a good idea to go from an exempt plan into something exposed to creditors. There's an overlap between needing the counsel of a good estate-planning attorney and needing a good creditor law attorney.

LIFE INSURANCE AND ANNUITIES. Most states also exempt the proceeds received by a beneficiary and frequently the cash value and annuity payments.

HOMESTEAD. As you might have read, there is some bankruptcy reform legislation in Congress that is expected to pass in the year 2000. Some of the versions would limit exempt equity in a house to $100,000. There remains the issue of whether Congress can override a state constitution that protects a homestead, and so this item merits close observation.

In some states, there is also a form of coownership called a "tenancy by the entirety." It is allowed only between spouses. A creditor can attach the property only if both spouses are liable for an obligation, not just one. Holding title in this way can offset a state's very low value exemption on the value of a house.

Protecting Nonexempt, or Nonqualified, Assets

These assets include stocks in brokerage accounts. The other day we had a physician walk in who had $3 million of securities in his personal name. The first thing we told him was to get that over to his spouse. He said, "What if we have a marital problem?" We told him: "Those are marital assets whether you have them in your name or not, and you're at a lot more risk of getting attacked by a creditor. Most judges in a divorce are going to treat those as marital assets, and they're 50-50 anyway." Nonexempt assets should go to the spouse with the least exposure.

OFFSHORE ASSET PROTECTION TRUSTS. Offshore asset protection trusts are getting a lot of press. U.S. jurisdictions are trying to get into the asset protection business as well, because they don't want to see that money leave the country. Places such as Alaska and Delaware

are starting to look at creating offshore asset protection *onshore,* since it is still uncertain whether one state will have to enforce the judgment of another state.

An important misconception is that offshore accounts can beat the IRS. Sorry, they aren't designed to do that. For U.S. tax purposes, an offshore asset protection trust is treated as a grantor trust, and a grantor trust is tax-neutral. The IRS taxes someone on a grantor trust as if he or she were still the owner.

The big difference is legal ownership in case of financial difficulties. Here's what makes them so good: If you get a judgment against you in the United States and these assets are in the other jurisdiction offshore, they don't recognize a U.S. judgment against you. In addition, there is secrecy by law for most of these jurisdictions. The employees of the bank or the trust company are subject to criminal prosecution under the laws of their country if they divulge any information. The point is that if a creditor does find out about an offshore trust, he or she may not be able to get the information necessary to find out how to sue it. The creditor will have to go to where the offshore trust is domiciled and hire someone and pay that person by the hour. The creditor probably will be inclined to settle for cents on the dollar because an offshore trust is so difficult to pursue.

Another key element that's important is statutes of fraud. If I know that I've got litigation filed or a judgment against me and then try to establish one of these trusts, it probably can be set aside. There are in-between gray areas where it still makes sense to do this, but if you are on the eve of having a problem, an offshore trust won't protect you. Often, foreign jurisdictions have a statute of limitations, and so if a trust has been in effect for one or two years, it can't be challenged.

In certain instances offshore asset protection trusts are great, but it's not a matter of one size fits all. These trusts can involve some significant expense; you need to know the practical aspects and do some due diligence. You may be worried about protecting yourself from a creditor when you really need to be worried about protecting yourself from the people you're giving the money to.

Exceptions

As always, there are exceptions to the rules. For instance, a home is not exempt from a mortgage or equity loan creditor. Among other exceptions are state taxes, alimony, and child support. The big exception that everyone can expect is federal income tax and the IRS. They can even attach retirement plan accounts.

For the most part, these exceptions come into play in the form of your obligations. We have been discussing protecting assets from abuse and flagrant loss, *not* hiding assets from one's responsibilities.

17

WEALTH REPLACEMENT TRUSTS

NOTHER "HIGH-END" TYPE OF PLANNING WORK that is common among top financial planners is the establishment of special trusts that enable wealth to transfer from one generation to the next.

One of the most famous stories in the estate-planning world dealt with the Halas family, owners of the Chicago Bears. Lack of planning subjected the Halas heirs to a tax bill of $90 million that was due within nine months. Stadiums and professional sports teams are not exactly liquid assets.

If you plan properly and take advantage of wealth replacement trusts, which typically are funded with life insurance, you can create enough liquid capital to assure your heirs the ability to pay the tax.

The IRS is not typically patient when it comes to large tax bills that result from the transfer of wealth. Although the government has been able to increase the amount of wealth excludable from tax, the bottom line is that at its highest level of exemption, $1 million, nearly all those who have acquired a fair amount of wealth will surpass this threshold.

Many younger readers might skip this chapter because they feel it does not apply to them, but that is often not true. Let's say you are in your midthirties and your net worth is over $1 million. Your net worth without any additions is likely to grow $8 million at just a 6 percent return by the time you are 70. If you live to 85, your net worth, again without any additions, could grow to over $16 million. The tax due without any planning could be more than $8 million to your heirs. If your estate grew at 8 percent, it would be worth $64 million with a whopping tax bill of over $32 million.

Most financial planners are very much aware of the burden heirs can assume during wealth transfer. Let's listen to some of the success stories and horror stories advisors have dealt with and see how wealth replacement trusts either solved or could have solved the problems.

WHAT IS YOUR OPINION ON THE ADVANTAGES AND DISADVANTAGES OF STRATEGIES SUCH AS WEALTH REPLACEMENT TRUSTS?

Lynn Hopewell believes wealth replacement trusts are missold. He usually mentions to clients that they can create more wealth at death by buying life insurance. He usually has a conversation with a clients that goes something like this: "Your estate will be $5 million, but $2 million will be paid in estate taxes. Your children will split the balance. If you think they should have more money, we will have to buy it with life insurance. You will have to pay for it every year, just like any other living expense." Lynn says that most clients respond, "Three million dollars is enough."

Glenn Kautt describes another form of protection that involves reducing or eliminating taxes on assets. In many cases clients have portfolios that exceed the unified credit allowance for estates. Even though this allowance will increase to a maximum of $1 million in the year 2006, many individuals' adjusted gross estates already exceed this amount. Many people forget that proceeds from an insurance policy are included in a taxable estate even if the money is paid to someone else. Since many people have insurance policies of $500,000 or more, it is quite easy to exceed the current unified credit limit.

The use of an irrevocable insurance trust, called by some the "wealth replacement" trust (WRT), is a popular tool for individuals with large estates. In cases where there will be estate taxes because of the size of the estate, the insurance proceeds go directly to the heirs.

Frequently, these trusts are combined with a charitable remainder trust (CRT), which will be discussed in the next chapter in more detail, where a gift is made to one or more charities by placing assets in the CRT. The individual making the gift to the charity removes the asset from the estate but gets current income from investments in the CRT. Furthermore, he or she may be able to get an extra tax benefit from selling highly appreciated assets placed in the CRT. Once an asset is inside the CRT, there is no tax from the sale of any asset.

To "replace" the assets (wealth) placed in the CRT, the WRT mentioned above is put in place with an insurance policy with a benefit equal to the value of the assets placed in the CRT. For example, for an estate of $3 million, a combination of a CRT of $1,500,000 and a WRT may be able to preserve $500,000 or more for the heirs.

Ray Ferrara points to WRTs as a very inexpensive way to provide for liquidity within an estate. Generally, the use of a second to-die policy (a life insurance policy that pays after the death of both of the insured parties) will help transfer wealth in a very tax-efficient way. Many of our professional clients are using irrevocable trusts funded with a life insurance policy on the life of the primary breadwinner. When the money is left in trust for the spouse and children, it stays outside the spouse's estate as well.

Kelley Schubert believes wealth replacement trusts and other trusts that are used in estate planning must be considered in each individual client's circumstances: "If the client has a sizable estate and is facing a 50 percent estate tax, it is wise to consider creating a trust outside the estate and funding that trust (whether it is with insurance premiums or some other vehicle) before the client dies. By doing this, the client is in essence receiving an estate tax deduction for the amount funded (assuming the annual exclusion can be used) as well as a deduction for any appreciation that occurs after funding (because the assets are no longer in the estate). If a life insurance policy is used as the vehicle for funding the trust, the appreciation inside the trust also accrues income tax–free if certain requirements are met. This can be a very powerful tool for retaining wealth that is passed down to children and grandchildren.

"If the annual exclusion cannot be used for the contributions to the trust, it is still better to make the contribution while the donor is alive and pay the gift tax due. This achieves two advantages. First, the money used to pay the gift tax is no longer in the estate; therefore, the donor has in essence received an estate tax deduction for the tax paid (this would not be the case if all taxes were paid at death). Second, any future appreciation in the gifted asset is now outside the estate and will avoid the 50 percent estate tax."

Wayne Caldwell explains that a WRT strategy was developed because of the significance estate tax has for the deterioration of a family's wealth: "I've recommended this strategy most often in the form of a second-to-die cash-value life insurance policy [similar to Ray Ferrara]. This insurance policy on the lives of the husband and the wife pays off only after the second death. It is typically owned by the children or an irrevocable life insurance trust. Either way, neither the cash value nor the death benefit is ever a part of the client's estate. At both of the insureds' deaths, it is passed to the heirs income tax–free and estate tax–free, helping to replace any lost wealth that had to be paid to the federal government."

Wayne states that this is a very effective strategy and allows high-net-worth individuals, by cash gifting to heirs (to pay the premiums) a small percentage of their net worth, to generate a substantial liquid cash benefit upon their death: "It combines some of the best of our wealth protection, estate-planning, and wealth transfer strategies. We use systematic gifting to transfer the dollars to make the premium payments. We use an irrevocable trust to get the asset out of the client's estate. We use life insurance that allows for income tax–free transfer to the beneficiary and the tax–free cash-value buildup inside the insurance policy, which is owned by the irrevocable life insurance trust. This cash value is not subject to any claims by creditors against either the parents or their heirs."

Wayne feels we are heading into a trend of reduced taxes in general and possibly reduced estate taxes. But he believes, regardless of any current or future tax changes, that this is a strategy well worth preserving.

John Bowen, Jr., sees these trusts as very attractive strategies, although many clients have difficulty understanding their application: "These trusts need to be part of an overall wealth management program and can significantly increase the probability of clients achieving their financial goals."

IS THERE A DOWNSIDE TO THIS STRATEGY?

Ray Ferrara reminded the group that a decision made and implemented today is irrevocable, whereas the tax laws may change in the future. The principal is forever out of reach. Also, if a client is uninsurable, the strategy may not work.

Glenn Kautt agrees that a downside to any irrevocable trust program is placing assets inside the trust: "These assets are irrevocably removed from the estate and also removed from the direct control of the original owner. While it is often possible for the original grantors to regain control of the assets if they want to, for successive beneficiaries this is not the case. In fact, often beneficiaries are prevented from gaining control or possession of trust assets for many years."

Harold Evensky adds relative poor performance as a downside to this type of strategy, as well as excessive costs, restricted options, and other unpleasant surprises.

Wayne Caldwell warns that any strategy that is irrevocable decreases flexibility and becomes a hard decision for clients. Any strategy that is heavily weighted toward controlling taxes runs the risk of not making sense if the tax rules change. He believes that strategies need to have something more than half their value coming from fundamental financial issues versus tax issues so that when tax changes come, it may not be quite as advantageous as it was, but it certainly will still make sense: "Any strategy that adds another layer of ownership, tracking, or accounting needs to be looked at carefully. The complexity needs to be balanced against the final value."

Overall, I agree with our experts. Wealth replacement is critical and minimizing estate taxes is preferable, but at what cost? I love my children more than anything in this world, but I tend to agree with Lynn Hopewell that if proper planning and an additional financial burden while you are living can increase their inheritance only nominally, is the planning worth the return? If you are in the situation just described, ask yourself, How much do I want to leave to my family or charity? If your goal can be accomplished without the use of trusts or without purchasing additional life insurance, then don't do it.

This may be a point of contention among many in the advisory field. The question would be, Even if you can leave the desired amount of money to your heirs, why not plan so that your favorite charity can get the money instead of the government? My response to this is that most charitable organizations are no better at distributing your funds than the government is. When you contribute to the largest charitable organizations in the United States, often only half or even less of your contribution ever makes it to the beneficiary. If the government gets the money, the hope is that a quarter of your funds will make it to something worthwhile.

My concluding point is that I believe in charitable causes and in establishing trusts and foundations that will help people live longer and help the unfortunate find opportunities. I also believe that all of us who achieve financial wealth have to be grateful to the country in which we live therefore responsible to contribute back to the system so that others, including my heirs, may share the opportunities I have had.

WEALTH TRANSFER

In the previous part on wealth preservation, we briefly described a couple ways to achieve wealth transfer. Since wealth preservation can mean both preserving personal wealth and preserving wealth for one's heirs, it is sometimes difficult to separate these topics.

In this final stage of wealth, we will focus on various estate-planning techniques to assure that your heirs receive the amount you planned. If you have a charitable intent, the evolution of charitable trust planning and specifically the "net income with make-up charitable trust" will be of particular interest.

18

CHARITABLE REMAINDER TRUSTS

WE TOUCHED PREVIOUSLY ON THE USE OF A CHAR-
ITABLE REMAINDER TRUST. A CRT can benefit
both the donor and the charitable organization;
however, the Tax Reform Act of 1997 dramatically limited some of the more creative charita-
ble trust planning techniques. As this vehicle can be very complex,
the following information provides only a foundation before consulting a qualified legal advisor.

Basically, a CRT is a tax-exempt trust to which a donor can contribute assets and, if all the requirements are met, receive an income
for life or a term of years as well as a gift tax charitable deduction. At
the end of the term or at the owner's death, the remaining assets pass
to one or more charitable organizations.

When this type of trust is set up in a will, the investor names another income beneficiary (probably one or all of his or her children). While the amount of the gift that made to the CRT is removed from the estate and therefore lessens the ultimate estate tax liability, the children are nevertheless disinherited to the extent of the gift to the CRT.

Two types of assets that are commonly gifted to charity are cash and securities. There are limits on the size of the retained income interest and the amount that is ultimately left to the charity. If you gift cash, your annual income tax deduction can be no more than 50 percent of your adjusted gross income. In other words, if your adjusted gross income is $100,000, the most you can take a deduction for in that year is $50,000. If, however, you decide to gift securities that have long-term capital gain, you are limited to a deduction of no more than 30 percent of your adjusted gross income. If you can't use the entire deduction during the first year, you can carry it forward five more years.

The use of such a trust can have multiple tax and nontax advantages to individuals who own substantially appreciated property. These advantages include a charitable deduction, resulting in reduced taxes; an increase in current cash flow; avoidance of capital gains upon the sale of appreciated property; the eventual reduction or elimination of estate taxes; and the satisfaction of knowing that property placed in the trust will eventually pass to charity.

A unitrust provides for the donor to receive annually a fixed percentage of the trust value (valued annually), whereas an annuity trust provides for the donor to receive a fixed amount. At the time the property is given to the trust, the donor can claim a current income tax deduction equal to the present value of the charity's remainder interest based on mortality expectations. Upon receipt of the gift, the trustee often sells the appreciated property and reinvests the proceeds to better provide the cash flow required to make the payments to the donor. This sale by the trust is usually free of any capital gains tax.

The biggest advantage I see in funding a CRT is having an asset removed from the estate. The second biggest reason is the current income tax deduction. The third reason is to provide a lifetime income stream to oneself and one's beneficiaries. Having said that, there is also a drawback to funding a CRT. The principal is forever removed from the investor's control. To make this type of program work, it is necessary to have charitable *intent*.

Who should consider a CRT? Anyone who has a charity or organization he or she would like to help; anyone who has an estate tax problem, that is, wealth that exceeds the unified credit exemption equivalent of $650,000; and anyone who has large capital gains on either stock or property.

An individual is currently entitled to pass $650,000 of wealth on to his or her heirs without any estate taxes. This is called a unified credit because it's unified between the estate and gift taxes together. If you make more than $650,000 in gifts or have more than $650,000 you're going to pass on through inheritance, your heirs will have to pay taxes starting at 37 percent.

The conventional approach to wealth planning is to keep more of what you earn and leave more of what you keep. This approach ignores the part that you can't keep, but with a charitable remainder trust, that's exactly what you address and gain control over—the social capital that goes out in estate taxes. This means capital that helps the welfare system, Social Security, the military, and so on. About 60 percent of state taxes go to the federal government for social reform. When you own a CRT, you can direct that social capital yourself. This way, you can have 100 percent of your gift stay in your town or state. If you want to control where the funds go, this type of planning offers the best opportunity to do that.

Here's how a charitable remainder trust works. This information was provided by Tom Nohr in his new book, *Financial Success in the Year 2000 and Beyond*.

As Tom explains, "The following example makes a lot of assumptions, but it's meant to illustrate the benefits of a CRT: Let's fast forward my life to the year 2030. By that time my wife and I would both be in our mid-sixties. Say we put $500,000 of highly appreciable ($100,000 cost basis) XYZ stock in a CRT. For that contribution, we get an income tax deduction of $126,000.

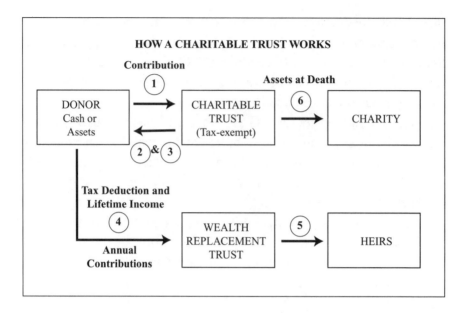

HOW A CHARITABLE TRUST WORKS

"The trust receives the stock and could sell it. Since the trust is a nontaxable entity, it does not pay any capital gains tax. Then it puts the proceeds into a variable annuity contract that will pay me and my wife an 8 percent return for life. When we die, the $500,000 or whatever amount is remaining goes to a named charity.

"At the same time, my wife and I create a wealth replacement trust, which is an irrevocable life insurance trust (ILIT or WRT), in the amount of $500,000. That costs us $6,000 a year to fund, which we can deduct from the $40,000 annual income we are receiving from the CRT, leaving us with $34,000 per year for living expenses. Then, when we die, the $500,000 in the ILIT goes to our children, federal and state income and estate tax–free. Aside from increasing our income and reducing our taxes, it also has the effect of diversifying our assets.

"What if, instead, we needed the $500,000 for living expenses? Our alternative would be to sell the stock piecemeal or, in a worst-case scenario, all in one year. In one year, we'd have to pay $80,000 in taxes—$400,000 ($500,000 less the $100,000 basis) times a 20 percent tax rate—and we would net $420,000.

"If we bought an annuity that gave us 8 percent of that a year, we'd receive $33,600 (less than we could get from the CRT). And then if we died, because a portion of our estate would be taxed at a minimum of 37 percent estate tax, we'd have to give another $155,000 of that $420,000 to the federal government. Our children would net only about $265,000."

To summarize, it is possible for a CRT to increase income, reduce taxes, diversify assets, and build wealth. At the same time, you're giving a charitable gift to an organization or cause you care about, and your heirs are potentially going to receive more money from the CRT than they would get if they received their inheritance in a more conventional way.

DO YOU DO ANY CHARITABLE PLANNING FOR YOUR CLIENTS? IF SO, WHAT TYPE AND WHAT ARE THE BENEFITS?

John Bowen, Jr., says that he does a significant amount of charitable planning and utilizes charitable remainder unit trusts, gift annuities, and private foundations. "It allows the client to achieve his or her charitable intent very cost-effectively."

Ray Ferrara often uses these trusts to save substantial amounts of taxes while providing a temporarily tax-favored cash flow. The client is often able to convert a highly appreciated asset with very little, if any, cash flow into a sufficient cash flow without incurring a capital gains tax on the conversion.

Kelley Schubert believes charitable planning should be discussed in every comprehensive estate-planning situation. "There are numerous types of charitable trusts that can be used to accomplish the client's objective while usually obtaining some tax benefit. If funded with the correct investment vehicle, some charitable trusts can be used to shift the taxation on investment earnings into a period of the client's life when the client's earnings from employment may be reduced or completely gone, thus subjecting the investment earnings to a lower tax rate.

"To determine if a charitable trust should be used for a client, there are a few questions that should be asked:

1. Does the client have a true charitable intent?
2. Does the client currently hold an asset that would receive favorable tax treatment if transferred to a charitable trust?
3. Are the potential benefits to be gained great enough to offset the accounting and legal costs of the setting up and maintenance of the trust?
4. How would using a charitable trust fit into the overall estate plan as well as asset protection needs?

"Each of these questions has important implications for whether a charitable trust should be used, what type of charitable trust to use, and how to fund the trust."

Harold Evensky believes charitable trusts allow clients to leverage their gifting by including Uncle Sam as a *codonor.* This is an interesting play on words. What I believe he is saying is that with proper planning, the government's share of one's wealth is actually donated to the charities of one's choice.

Wayne Caldwell feels this is one of the most satisfying aspects of the client-advisor relationship: "Substantial gifts create a reduction in the estate for estate tax purposes and can reduce current income tax as well as create a charitable deduction that can be deducted from future income."

He has created charitable planning programs that have left substantial monies in a donor-advised fund at the community foundation. The significant tax deductions retrieved dollars that were going to be lost to Washington, D.C., but instead were put back into the community. He has also replaced the lost wealth by using a wealth replacement trust. In the end, the heirs received as much as or more than they would have received without this strategy.

Wayne shared a specific client situation involving a real estate asset with a very low basis and a very high capital gain potential. He showed the client how a CRT might function. In the end, a very substantial CRT was created with specific donor-advised instructions.

The problematic real estate asset was liquidated without any capital gains, and a very rewarding relationship was established with the local area foundation. The clients started down a path of very focused, organized charitable activities that brought them a great deal of satisfaction.

This brings us back to the conclusion of the previous chapter. This couple was very charitably inclined and found great pleasure in making contributions. This should be the driving factor behind the establishment of such a trust, not trying to find a loophole.

19

ESTATE-PLANNING TECHNIQUES

THIS CHAPTER CONCLUDES THE INFORMATION CONTENT **OF THIS BOOK** with a discussion by our panel of financial advisors of the estate-planning techniques they use to assure that clients and their heirs fully enjoy the effort they have put forth to achieve financial freedom. While no two situations are identical and many of the techniques are innovative, what follows are general estate-planning ideas that will be relevant to the majority of readers.

Imagine you worked hard all your life and amassed a sizable net worth, but because you hadn't taken the time to understand estate planning, your family ended up with only 50 cents of each of your hard-earned dollars. You would never have agreed to an outcome like that on any other business decisions, but when you die, if your financial affairs are not in order, more than half your wealth can go to the IRS and beneficiaries you didn't choose. A lifetime of great efforts and good investments can be undone by no or poor predeath or disability planning.

This chapter is designed to help you see estate planning and the concepts introduced in previous chapters in a new light. The hope is that you can enjoy the fruits of your labors and be assured that your appointed beneficiaries will receive what you intended, unburdened by complicated legal hassles and severe tax penalties.

The most basic elements of estate planning are *who* will get *what* of yours upon your death and *how* and *when* they will get it. It sounds simple enough, right? Unfortunately, no, especially if the total value of your assets exceeds the previously discussed current unified credit equivalent of $650,000 (indexed).

Variables such as how you hold title to your assets, how you document your intentions, whether you have equity assets or tax-deferred assets, whether you have a surviving spouse, and which of your assets will provide retirement income are all major factors to address in estate planning and require scrutiny of the many possible tax implications.

Today it is possible for do-it-yourselfers to write their own wills or create a trust without the help and expense of professionals and specialists. Software packages, how-to books, and tutorials are available to assist the ambitious individual. However, if you fall prey to procrastination or become overwhelmed, chances are that the information you use won't include the complexities of the tax laws or that you won't make the adjustments needed to follow changes in the tax laws.

All your do-it-yourself thoroughness can be nullified if, for example, your beneficiaries die in the wrong order! In short, the money spent on the advice and handling of a specialist is well worth the comprehensive consideration to details an effective estate plan requires. Of course, you'll still have to make the decisions and supply the details.

Back to beneficiaries. How do you want the beneficiaries to receive assets from your estate: by transfer of ownership, in a lump sum, or by payments over a period of time? Each beneficiary could have different payout arrangements. Some people are concerned about spendthrift children or their children's spouses. In that case, specific instructions or distribution vehicles can leave them with more economic security and more money over time.

GET IT IN WRITING

Once you've determined the who and what, you need to select the proper tools for transferring your assets. If you don't have a will, the distribution of your assets after taxes will be done according to the statutes of the state in which you die or have property. A will is necessary to ensure that your intentions are carried out the way you want them to be. However, the will must go through probate, a court process in front of a judge to establish the validity of the will, which can take a lot of time and be fairly expensive to execute.

Once you've written a will, it must be continually updated to account for any additions or deletions of assets as well as any beneficiary changes or tax-law changes. What if your spouse dies before you do? How will that affect your estate and the apportionment to any other beneficiaries?

Don't be fooled into thinking that having a will is the last word on the subject! If you own anything as "joint tenants with rights of survivorship" or live in a "community property" state, that title will supersede a will. If we own an asset ourselves and we die, even if we're married, the asset goes through probate before it's transferred to the rightful heir. If we own as joint tenants with rights of survivorship, the surviving joint tenant, usually a spouse, can just fill out the proper form and have the ownership changed to his or her name only.

Did you know your will can be contested? The way you hold title to your assets and the manner in which you transfer those assets make a big difference in the effectiveness of your will, to say nothing of the tax consequences.

You have several different choices of how to transfer your assets to your heirs, and every decision you make will have some tax consequences. Aside from income tax, estate tax starts at 37 percent, and generation-skipping transfer tax (GSTT) starts at 55 percent! But there are also the exemptions and credits we discussed before. It's common to have changes in tax laws that require an adjustment in an estate plan to avoid or take advantage of those changes. While this is obviously an ongoing process of diligence, there are some facts that can help in the initial planning.

Let's turn to the issue of a step-up in basis at death. After death, equity assets receive a "step-up in basis" valuation at the time of transfer of ownership. Examples of these assets are stocks, real estate, and a family business. Any asset whose value is likely to grow—where you would typically have capital gains taxes when you sell it—would normally qualify for a step-up in basis.

The step-up is simply that the current value at the time of transfer becomes the new owner's basis for capital gains calculations. *The exception:* If ownership is transferred through joint tenancy with rights of survivorship, the surviving owner's cost basis is the original basis on 50 percent of the asset and the stepped-up value on the transferred 50 percent of the asset.

Think of it this way: The day you die becomes the day of the "sale" of your assets. You no longer own them, and they become the property of your designated heirs. Dividends and capital gains taxes are assessed as of that day and are due and payable from your estate. The new owners of your assets are assessed an inheritance tax on the current value of those assets. At the time the new owners sell the asset, they are liable for the capital gains taxes on any growth from the value at which they acquired the asset.

Qualified retirement vehicles such as IRAs and annuities are tax-deferred. That means the investor has not paid any income tax on the dollars invested in those vehicles. When those assets are transferred to the investor's heirs, the heirs are liable for the income tax and the estate tax. Unfortunately, an investor trades tax deferral for a step-up in basis.

Bonds, certificates of deposit, savings accounts, and other forms of cash have little to no capital gain and amount to a basic transfer of cash to the heirs. This transfer is still subject to probate, just like other assets.

The death benefit from a life insurance policy is generally 99.9 percent free of income tax, although there are some exceptions for business uses. If you own a policy through a trust or if your heirs own it, there is no estate tax on it and they get dollar for dollar. Life insurance sometimes is the only asset guaranteed to provide cash at exactly the right time—at death.

Begin by checking how you own, or hold title to, all your existing assets and documents and see if anything needs to be updated. Review everything periodically because situations change. The rule of thumb is to review your estate plan every time there's a major transaction or a change in your life or no less than every two years. Another suggestion is get a legal review each year just to make sure you are getting the maximum advantage from the current tax law.

Every time you add an asset to your estate, make certain to place it in the proper ownership and name beneficiaries, if appropriate. Say you receive a check for $20,000 and decide to open a stock account. You've set up a trust, but you didn't bring the trust documents or your spouse, and so you just put it in your name. Then you put off properly transferring this investment until you forget about it. Your estate plan will not protect that asset.

If you own something, even if you are married, the asset will go through probate before going to the rightful heir. However, if you own something as joint tenants or as community property *with rights of survivorship,* the survivor just fills out the proper documents and gets 100 percent ownership.

After a spouse has died, many people put their children on the title of their equity assets as joint tenants with rights of survivorship because of the automatic transfer. Essentially, when they are put on as joint tenants with rights of survivorship, you are making a gift. Instead of making the transfer easier, this results in an income tax problem and a gift tax problem.

For example, if you own $1 million of Microsoft stock and put a child on that account with joint rights of survivorship, you technically gave the child half the account—in tax language, a half million dollar gift. Then, when you die, the child gets a step-up in basis on only half the account.

Even with a spouse, sometimes it's not good to leave everything outright. Couples frequently have what are called "sweetheart" wills. If the husband dies first, he gives everything to her, and if the wife dies first, she gives everything to him. That's okay with small estates whose value is less than the $650,000 exemption, but what if the estate is worth more than that? If, instead, the couple put their assets into the proper trust so that at the first death the estate is split in two, the $650,000 unified credit exemption equivalent can be used for each individual.

For example, in an estate worth $900,000, the decedent's half is $450,000, which is less than the tax credit equivalent of $650,000. Now, at the second death, the survivor's estate is also only $450,000; therefore, there is no tax.

Holding assets in one or more trusts can serve many purposes, from avoiding probate to minimizing and eliminating certain taxes. A major goal of estate planning is to position wealth so that it appears smaller to the IRS; that way, when you die, it won't take as much tax. One of the easiest ways to do that is to leave everything to charity. Then, in the eyes of the IRS, the estate is worth zero. Another way is through gifting. If you start gifting $11,000 a year now to your children, this principal amount and all its growth are not included in the estate.

Irrevocable trusts actually diminish the size of an estate in the eyes of the IRS. *Irrevocable* means that one can't get it back, can't undo it, and can't change it. Irrevocable trusts are commonly combined with life insurance. If you buy $1 million of life insurance and pay the premiums, when you die, the IRS wants part of that million. If a trust buys life insurance on your life, when you die, there will be no income tax or estate tax on that million dollars of insurance.

A charitable trust, a form of irrevocable trust, is a way to retain income from an estate and get tax advantages by making the charitable gift now. There is also what's called a GRIT, which is a retained income trust; a GRANT, which is a retained annuity trust; and a GRUNT, which is a retained unit trust.

A qualified personal residence trust (QPRT) is a way to irrevocably give away your house to your children over a period of years, usually 10 years or longer, for a fraction of its worth today. Because you are not making a gift for 10 years, you can get a discount on the value in the future, and then all the growth is also outside the estate and is transferred to the children after so many years.

We briefly mentioned the GSTT, the tax you pay for giving your assets to your grandchildren instead of to your children. However, each person has a $1 million exemption. You can set up a trust, put a million dollars in it, and fill out the right paperwork, and that million dollars is always exempt from GSTT. This is allocated on Form 709 for the IRS. If that million dollars grows to be $10 million before you die, the entire $10 million is free from GSTT because you allocated it when you gave the million.

PRECAUTIONARY MEASURES

A will goes into effect when you die; it's not a document that can take care of you when you're living. A will doesn't help if you become incompetent.

If you become disabled or incompetent and cannot manage your own financial affairs or even make your own health care decisions, a properly documented plan on how you want things carried out will ensure the execution of your intentions without disruption. A *durable power of attorney* usually is used for financial matters; the term *durable* means it will last. It's sometimes called a "springing" power of attorney. Most people don't just grant an open power of attorney; they make a provision in which it springs into being when needed and is durable, or long-lasting.

Some institutions will not accept durable powers of attorney and health care powers of attorney if they are "outdated." It's important to know the rules and stay on top of any changes. Some states are updating their laws, giving people more options and ways to use those documents.

The best scenario for an incompetent person is to have a guardian and a conservator and have all the person's money in a trust where it can be managed for that person without disruption.

In a health care directive or health care power of attorney, you can even set up your own parameters to determine incompetence. For example, if two doctors agree that you're mentally incompetent, the power of attorney springs into effect.

In the case of a husband and wife, everything is usually owned as joint tenants with rights of survivorship, and the spouse automatically makes health care decisions. What will happen if your spouse is already gone? If you haven't designated a guardian and a conservator in writing and don't have a power of attorney in place, even your own children will have to go through living probate, or the court will appoint someone. It's common for people to change title to their assets to joint tenancy with survivorship with their children when their health begins to go and they need to preserve assets. These are all things you need to think about and prepare for regardless of how uncomfortable it makes you, because you get no second chances in these matters.

Summary Checklist

- Who will get your money after your death?
- Do they receive a lump sum, or do they get payments over a period of time? List each beneficiary and any requirements.
- Which of your assets are better to leave to your heirs, and which should you spend before you die?
- How will your money be managed if you become incompetent or disabled and can't manage your own financial affairs?
- Who will make your health care decisions?

WHAT IS THE BEST WAY TO TRANSFER WEALTH TO FUTURE GENERATIONS?

Glenn Kautt says there is no single "best" way to transfer assets to future generations: "The transfer techniques used will depend on the individual financial and personal situation of those involved, the amount and characteristics of the assets, the number and ages of the people involved, the amount of time available to transfer assets, and the income and estate tax consequences of each possible transfer technique. Choose a transfer technique that is simple and flexible, such as annual gifting."

However, for very large estates, such as those in excess of $10 million, where there are multiple generations, assets of different types located in several states, and so forth, Glenn recommends a combination of techniques.

One technique Glenn has used is a family limited partnership (FLP) in combination with revocable and irrevocable trusts. If an FLP is properly constructed and managed, assets may be transferred to it at a discounted value. This effectively raises the annual amount that may be placed in the trust, accelerating the transfer of wealth. The IRS has repeatedly challenged the discount but essentially has lost every case taken to court: "Our clients who are using this technique have received discounts of 35 to 45 percent on assets, including mutual funds and stocks."

Glenn continues: "An irrevocable trust is used to immediately remove a substantial amount of assets from a large estate. This trust can be used in conjunction with a CRT and may serve as the owner of insurance for the wealth replacement technique discussed earlier.

"For one particular client, the combination of techniques discussed has decreased the overall estate tax over $1 million to date. By the time the original grantors are 80 years old, we estimate the total tax savings will be in excess of $9 million. To assure compliance with all laws and reduce the risk from IRS challenges, we engage top estate-planning attorneys and accountants to prepare documents and tax returns."

Lynn Hopewell believes the best way to transfer wealth is to give it away: "There are many techniques. Annual gifting works well. Sometimes, if there is enough money, giving away the unified credit amounts will get appreciation out of an estate. Family limited partnerships seem to be working well in getting discounts on gifts and estates."

John Bowen, Jr., agrees that there is no single right way to pass wealth to future generations: "It depends on the type of asset and how one wants it to be passed on. For example, with real property, a family limited partnership can be extremely attractive."

Ray Ferrara says, "Where appropriate, a dynasty trust is a powerful tool to provide estate and GSTT tax-free transfer of assets to more than one generation beneath us while protecting the assets from our children's and grandchildren's creditors or ex-spouses. Often, a conventional IRA can be passed down several generations [subject to RMD (Required Minimum Distribution) rules] using this method." Depending on the situation, he has found that a combination of a family limited partnership, gifting trust, generation-skipping trust, wealth replacement trust, and GRAT (Grantor Retained Annuity Trust) are powerful tools.

Kelley Schubert's opinion is, "The best way to transfer wealth to future generations is by using a method that provides a low estate and income tax burden, is relatively free from creditors' claims against the assets, controls the distribution of the wealth in accordance with the donor's wishes, and is not too complex or cost-prohibitive to administer.

"To accomplish all these goals, some combination of gifts, trusts, partnerships, and insurance is probably the answer."

Wayne Caldwell says he has two rules that cover everyone: "You must plan wealth transfers as carefully as you've planned wealth accumulation. Lack of or improper planning is the greatest detriment to successful wealth transfers. Even basic estate planning is a highly procrastinated event. With the complexities and potential confusion over advanced estate planning, and with lifetime wealth transfer techniques added in, it can overwhelm even the most sophisticated clients.

"The next wealth transfer rule that should be used by every family is that the individual or couple who are looking at their wealth transfer planning options must look at the family as a financial unit. As most people know, there are specific rules regarding transfers between husband and wife, parents and children, and grandparents and grandchildren. Great wealth transfer planning by the senior family members can quickly deteriorate in one generation because of poor planning at the children's level. This view of the family as a financial unit starts with the selection of a successor trustee, either a family member or a professional, and continues with deciding between outright gifts to heirs and gifts in trusts. These difficult and at times emotional decisions create a stressful decision-making atmosphere for the client. A team consisting of a financial advisor, a tax accountant, and an attorney, all of whom are knowledgeable about estate planning, working closely together on a client's behalf often is the only hope for a client and his or her family to resolve these issues. Clients need to establish relationships with these professionals now so that they can begin and complete their estate planning as soon as possible."

IS THERE A DOWNSIDE TO THIS STRATEGY?

Ray Ferrara hints that few attorneys understand the strategy and that the few who have the know-how are expensive. From the client's perspective, it can all get to be too complicated and lead to frustration.

Lynn Hopewell cautions that one has to be careful not to give away too much too soon. Trusts and limited partnerships have a certain cost, administrative complexity, and overhead.

Glenn Kautt talks about the risk of any gifting program not accomplishing all that it is intended to. It may not transfer enough assets before the death of the grantors. The strategy may transfer so much money that it puts the grantor at financial risk by not having enough assets to cover a financial emergency: "We consider these risks in developing the program. In most cases, we recommend protecting the grantors during their lifetime rather than gifting so much that it puts them at financial risk. Properly constructed and managed irrevocable trusts and FLPs do just that."

Wayne Caldwell affirms that estate and wealth transfer planning is a very intimate process. Every aspect, both financial and personal, of a family's situation needs to be addressed. There is a spectrum of emotional issues, ranging from the financial competence of individual family members to basic belief systems regarding blood relatives versus nonblood relatives.

CAN YOU GIVE AN EXAMPLE OF A
SUCCESSFUL ESTATE PLAN?

Ray Ferrara has a client who recently sold his business and ended up with a net worth after taxes of approximately $15 million. He had done virtually no estate planning. By setting up a family limited partnership, which is owned by his new living trust, he probably will be able to take a discount for gift and estate taxes that conservatively will approach 25 to 30 percent of his FLP. He then made a gift of the FLP interest to a gifting trust, which provides enough cash to pay a premium for a second-to-die life insurance policy within the wealth replacement trust. The client did this on a split-dollar basis in which the wealth replacement trust owns the life insurance but the gifting trust owns the cash value. Therefore, the cash value is still available to the gifting trust for future use, if needed.

Ray also used a GRAT over a seven-year period to transfer a significant part of the estate and not use any of the lifetime exemption. By putting into the GRAT highly appreciating assets, the client probably will be able to pass a significant amount of money to the next generation.

Wayne Caldwell used the same family as an example in an earlier question, and it is certainly appropriate to use it again here. Once the decision was made by the family to enter formal estate planning, a commitment to do it right and completely was shared by the parents and children. This became evident early on with the children's commitment to understanding and accepting their responsibility as successor trustees. Wayne cautions clients that selecting one of their children as a successor trustee appears to be an easy choice. However, successor trustee relations can get very complex when the parents become unwilling or unable to handle their affairs during their lifetime and the children must step in on their behalf.

This family was looked at as a financial unit, and they were all actively involved in the process. Basic estate planning was put into place, wealth replacement trusts were established, systematic annual gifting was arranged, and a major charitable donation and the creation of a donor-advised fund with the local area foundation were completed. The charitable intent of this donor-advised fund was established by the parents, with latitude given to the children for ongoing implementation.

Although at the time both parents were in reasonably good health, only three years after everything had been put into place the husband died. Shortly thereafter, the wife became unwilling to handle her affairs and allowed the successor trustees to step in. At the husband's death, the wife, with counsel and strong family communications, decided to use disclaimers to allow the assets of her deceased husband to pass directly to the children. She also transferred real estate assets to the children, relieving her of any personal responsibilities.

WHAT TOOLS DO YOU USE—SOFTWARE, CHARTS, WORKSHEETS—TO ANALYZE A CLIENT'S WEALTH TRANSFER OPTIONS?

Kelley Schubert uses a spreadsheet that contains certain assumptions that can be changed easily, plus financial- and estate-planning software from Mobius. For annuity analysis, he uses Aegon's proprietary software.

Glenn Kautt uses a combination of commercial estate tax and planning software with proprietary worksheets to frame the discussions and design and implement the overall estate plan. In addition, he works with highly qualified attorneys and accountants to devise estate plans.

Lynn Hopewell doesn't do too much in this area, and so he doesn't have some of the specialized software, such that designed for charitable giving techniques: "Spreadsheets do the job for us when we need them."

Ray Ferrara uses VISTA 2.1, Kettley, and Leonard software for estate planning.

Unfortunately, most of these tools are not available to consumers. An investor must work with a qualified financial advisor to benefit from these estate- and investment-planning tools.

CONCLUSION

IHAVE BEEN IN THE BUSINESS OF CREATING AND DISTRIBUTING INVESTMENT PRODUCTS for over 11 years, and I have to admit that this project was very educational for me. As I read this book over, I think of topics that have not been addressed. The areas of offshore funding, hedge funds within insurance wraps, and qualified investments for accredited investors are absent from this book. I would like to think that this book is a very comprehensive guide for investors who are beginning the journey of wealth accumulation as well as many who have achieved wealth and are interested in learning about ways to distribute and transfer it.

My objective in the future will be to take the steps necessary to help my clients move from being a comfortably wealthy investor to having a degree of wealth that is achieved only by a very small percentage of people. For 99 percent of us, this book will supply the tools and guidance needed to achieve dreams far in excess of most. Although at times the advisors' responses to the questions were short, in many cases there was an interesting "one-liner" that proved valuable. I want to thank all the advisors for taking the time to respond to my questions. I hope that the information and the format in which they were relayed are helpful in achieving your goal of financial wealth.

WEALTH MAKERS INDEX

IN THIS APPENDIX you will get to know our panel of financial experts. Not only will you find out how to reach them, some of them will share the success stories that gave them the most satisfaction.

Lynn Hopewell, CFP
The Monitor Group, Inc.
12450 Fair Lakes Circle, Suite 650
Fairfax, VA 22033
(703) 968-3002/(703) 968-3005 (fax)
hopewell@monitor-inc.com

Lynn started in the financial services business in August 1980, when he joined Donald Rembert in a partnership. Three years later he converted to fee-only compensation and in 1990 he started an independent firm, The Monitor Group, Inc. In 1999 he merged with Kautt Financial Services, Inc. Today they have a 10-employee firm that manages about $170 million.

What prompted Lynn to enter the business? He was looking for a new career. He had grown tired of engineering and government contracting and wanted to work with people in his community and run his own show. He read a story in *Money Magazine* on the new profession of financial planning and was hooked. Today Lynn enjoys the technical challenges of financial planning and feels his Harvard MBA prepared him for the job.

His specialty within the context of investment management? Lynn says he does his best work in retirement planning and in creating retirement capital analysis models and implementing them. Lynn is currently working on expanding that research to explicitly address the uncertainty in such models.

Most Satisfying Success Story
Lynn had a client couple who had the opportunity to liquidate a large number of stock options that had increased in value far beyond their expectations. They were torn between squeezing the last drop out of the rise in stock prices and the inevitable fluctuations in price, which could as easily have declined and removed a large part of their gains. After an extensive tax and cash-flow analysis, Lynn advised them to cash in their options in two separate blocks. The couple retired at ages 37 and 32!

Glenn G. Kautt, CFP, EA
The Monitor Group, Inc.
12450 Fair Lakes Circle, Suite 650
Fairfax, VA 22033
(703) 968-3002/(703) 968-3005 (fax)
kautt@monitor-inc.com

Glenn started in the financial services business consulting to small business owners in 1981. He merged his practice with a financial-planning firm in 1984 and became a certified financial planner in 1987. Along with other professionals, he bought the assets of the firm and formed a large planning practice. He left that firm in the early 1990s to become a fee-only planner.

What prompted Glenn to enter the business? A strong desire to solve difficult problems and work directly with people.

Glenn's specialty is retirement and estate planning.

Harold Evensky, CFP
241 Sevilla Avenue
Coral Gables, FL 33134
(305) 448-8882
harold@evensky.com

Harold started in the financial services business with Bach (now Prudential Securities) in 1981. He entered the business because he was facing a career change and saw an advertisement for Bach in the paper. It sounded fascinating.

His specialty is wealth management and financial planning.

John J. Bowen, Jr., President and CEO
Assante Capital Management
1190 Saratoga Avenue, Suite 200
San Jose, CA 95129
(408) 260-3110
jbowen@rwb.com

John started in the financial services business by joining his predecessor firm, Reinhardt & Associates, in May 1978. This was one of the first firms to focus on financial planning for individuals.

John always enjoyed finance. His undergraduate degree was in economics, and he looked for an area where he could apply his knowledge to help individuals reach their financial goals. The non-career benefits of the financial services industry were particularly attractive. He interviewed with a number of wire houses and insurance companies and chose to go with a small boutique firm that he thought would give much more personal service to clients and would really accomplish financial planning.

Initially he was a general practitioner, but he was fortunate enough to begin practicing in Silicon Valley. It became very clear that he would be working with many affluent clients. There was a significant need for tax planning in the early 1980s. John subsequently received an MBA with a tax concentration so that he could focus on this area.

Most Satisfying Success Story
"There is nothing more satisfying than to have clients who have achieved success and are extremely satisfied with the aid I provided them in the process. I think of some of the retirement parties and weddings I've attended where I've been introduced as 'the financial advisor who made this all possible.' Clearly, it was the client who earned the money. I do believe my focus on helping them make smart decisions and providing them with peace of mind dramatically increased the probability of their reaching their financial goals."

John told us how easy it is to get caught up in the entrepreneurial drain, especially living in Silicon Valley. He has many investors with high-tech stock options or founders stock. Often these assets reach values far beyond their owners' expectations. John has a strategy of helping his clients discover what would be a reasonable amount of compensation for a stock option or founders stock. Seeing these values achieved is extremely exciting to him. More important, however, he often gets clients to diversify and take some of their holdings to start building a portfolio outside the one stock. He teaches them how to build a portfolio that is capable of helping them achieve financial independence. In several cases, if his clients had not sold some of their company stock early, they never would have realized any gains. John feels it is the *advice* that makes the difference between financial independence and starting over.

V. Raymond Ferrara, CFP, President
ProVise Management Group, Inc.
611 Druid Road East, Suite 105
Clearwater, FL 33756
(727) 441-9022 or (800) 633-3049
(727) 449-1625 (fax)
ferrara@provise.com

Ray started in the financial services business in April 1971 on a part-time basis while working with IBM to sell mainframe computers at NASA Goddard Space Flight Center. He decided to become licensed, hoping that he might be able to further his education in investment planning. After working in the business for only four months, Ray found himself earning more doing financial planning part-time than he was making selling computers full-time. Ray said it didn't take a rocket scientist to figure out the rest, and so in September 1971, he left IBM and entered the business full-time. He hasn't looked back since.

Ray's specialty is asset management, estate planning, and financial planning.

Most Satisfying Success Story

Ray helped one couple start an education fund for their daughter. Over the years they were encouraged to increase what started out as a $50 per month check-o-matic program. One day the couple invited Ray to their daughter's graduation party. At the party the young graduate stood up in front of everyone and thanked her parents for all their help and support. She then turned to Ray and said, "I also want to thank Mr. Ferrara for making sure that my parents saved for my education. Without his help, we would not have been able to afford my college education." Talk about success!

Ray adds, "Perhaps the most important thing that we do well is what we call investor management, that is, keeping clients' expectations in line with reality and keeping them from doing the wrong thing at the wrong time."

Thomas Muldowney, CFP
1625 East State Street
PO Box 4354
Rockford, IL 61110-0854
(815) 227-0300
Tmuldowney@savant-capital.com

Thomas started in the financial services business in August 1974. He had graduated from college into one of the worst economies ever. There were wage and price controls, the oil embargo, and the worst financial economy since October 1929. He needed a job, and the insurance companies were the only ones that would hire him.

Thomas's specialty is listening carefully to determine what a client means, which may differ remarkably from what the client says.

Marilyn R. Bergen, CFP
PO Box 69468
4800 SW Macadam Avenue, Suite 100
Portland, OR 97201
(503) 227-5284
cmcinvest@aol.com
www.cmcinvest.com

Marilyn started in the financial services business in 1982 because she was fascinated by the ability to help people establish financial goals and come up with solutions to their problems.

Her specialty is investment management and retirement planning; however, she believes her real specialty is her ability to listen to clients, ask questions to determine what is truly important to them, help them clarify the areas that are problems, and work with them to find solutions that match their values.

Most Satisfying Success Story

A couple had multiple financial planning needs, and so she began by educating them about the merits of including equities in a long-term portfolio. When they started working together, the clients had many individual bonds and bond mutual funds, but only about 10 percent of the portfolio was invested in the stock market. Because the clients were only in their forties, Marilyn helped them focus on their need to have their portfolio grow for a potentially long-term retirement. She showed them what rate of return over inflation they'd need to achieve on the basis of their current circumstances and desires. They began to invest in equities over a period of time with both existing money and annual additions to the portfolio. In conjunction with the retirement planning, they completed college planning for their two young children and set up a fund for potential emergencies, plus additional liquidity for "opportunities." As the years progressed, Marilyn combined their profit sharing with a money purchase plan so that they could fund the maximum amount possible in any chosen year. Next she recommended that any excess money be placed in a variable annuity for tax-deferred growth and to provide a portion of their retirement savings.

Over the years Marilyn worked with their attorney and reviewed their values and circumstances, life insurance, and disability insurance coverage; had conversations related to rental properties and potential real estate purchases; and discussed college selections for their children.

Although she has other clients who are wealthier from a balance sheet perspective, these clients stand out in her mind as her greatest success. They were the ideal clients, always willing to be educated about new financial-planning issues. They have stayed the course during downturns and are much wealthier as a result. They understand that all aspects of their financial life are interrelated and call her to discuss any financial decisions before they make final plans. They have been willing to spend the time necessary to keep up to date on the "big financial-planning picture."

Kelley Schubert, CPA, CFP, President
Summit Asset Management, Inc.
400 Chisholm Place, Suite 110
Plano, TX 75075
(972) 422-1010
(972) 881-1395 (fax)

Kelley started in the financial services business in 1993, when he received his Series 7 securities license. He was a practicing CPA, and part of his responsibility was to create a historical record of financial transactions, often involving investments. He found that clients' actual after-tax returns were frequently much lower than what they expected and came to realize there was a need for more truthful and accurate communication between investment advisor and client, along with a more tax-efficient investment approach that would not sacrifice earning potential.

Kelley specializes in enabling clients to make the right decisions, free of emotional bias, and in supplying perspective for the correct historical information through education, communication, and relationships. Most people who fail to achieve their investment goals do so not because they bought the wrong investment but because they systematically made the wrong decisions about what might have been the right investment. These wrong decisions usually could have been avoided with a little bit of proper investor education and a lot of weeding out of the emotional element of the decision.

Kim Foss-Erickson, CFP, President, and CEO
E & A Investment Advisory, Inc.
3300 Douglas Boulevard, Suite 420
Roseville, CA 95661
(916) 786-7626
(916) 773-3287 (fax)
EAInvest@aol.com

Kim started in the financial services business in December 1989. Early in her career she worked as an assistant to a broker at Birr Wilson and later worked as a financial advisor with Merrill Lynch. In 1989 she became frustrated by the conflict of interest inherent in a commission-based sales environment and founded E & A Investment Advisory, Inc., a fee-only registered investment firm that is based on integrity and creates an environment in which clients' interests and financial goals are paramount.

Kim's firm was founded on the principle that an effective investment portfolio directly reflects the investor's primary economic objective. She strives to achieve a target rate of return, subject to a calculated level of risk, for each investor. She specializes in long-term investment strategy and dynamic portfolio design customized to each client's financial needs.

Joe Campisi, EA, CFP, ATA
HD Vest
1036 Valley Forge Road
Norristown, PA 19403
(610) 630-9277

Joe started in the financial services business with a tax service in 1980, doing financial planning as an incidental service to his tax practice. Not being licensed to implement products, he referred clients to someone who could help them or had clients carry out the implementation themselves. Joe wasn't always happy with the end results, and so he became a registered rep in 1991 and an advisor in 1992.

Joe's speciality is professional money management service based on modern portfolio theory, with estate planning as a secondary focus.

Stan Hargrave, CFP
3714 Tibbetts Street, Suite 100
Riverside, CA 92506
(909) 781-7320

Stan started in the financial services business in 1973. He had known since high school that he would become an advisor. His specialty is wealth management.

Patrick Moran
3200 East Camelback Road, Suite 245
Phoenix, AZ 85018
(602) 954-8300

Pat started in the financial services business in April 1986 as a result of his own investment experiences. His specialty is investment and retirement planning.

Lance A. Pelky
Lance Pelky & Associates, Inc.
9171 Towne Centre Drive, Suite 435
San Diego, CA 92122
(858) 623-9570 or (800) 746-1100
(858) 623-9572 (fax)

Lance started in the financial services business in 1985, knowing he wanted to help people accumulate and maintain wealth. His specialty is retirement planning, generating monthly income, and reducing investment taxes.

Tom J. Nohr, CFP, RFC
Tom Nohr & Associates
20632 Redwood Road, Suite E
Castro Valley, CA 94546
(888) 376-7171
tomnohr@pacbell.net

Tom started in the financial services business in August 1985, wanting to help people provide for their future. His specialty is efficient tax savings and distribution planning for retirement.

Most Satisfying Success Story
Tom's barber, a man who had cut his hair for twenty-one years, said to him, "Tom, I've noticed that all my friends have nothing for their years of work. I am so glad you had me put money away each month, because without your persistence I would also have nothing."

Tom told a couple who simply wanted to own their own home exactly what was needed. Because of his advice, their house is being constructed today instead of five years from now.

Floyd L. Shilanski, RFC, RFP
431 West Seventh Avenue, Suite 100
Anchorage, AK 99501
(907) 278-1351
floyd@shilanski.com

Floyd started in the financial services business in 1978 because he felt ripped off by a financial planner and CPA and decided to do something to help other people avoid that experience. His specialty is motivating people to take charge of their lives.

Most Satisfying Success Story
One of Floyd's clients, a couple in their midforties, had accumulated a good nest egg but wanted to spend more time together rather than watching over their money. They both had great jobs and salaries with a local office of a large international company. The wife was a cancer survivor, and they were looking to get out of the cold and spend some quality time together. The three of them developed a plan to get the couple out of Alaska in ten years.

About a year into the plan, their employer went through a downsizing. Floyd positioned some bailout money from current assets so that they could travel for 36 months without touching their retirement funds. They were actually able to travel for almost five years without touching their nest egg, and now they live very comfortably in sunny Arkansas.

Wayne O. Caldwell, CFP, RFC, President and Senior Principal
Premier Financial Group, Inc.
725 Sixth Street
Eureka, CA 95501
(707) 443-2741 or (800) 331-7212
(707) 443-9411 (fax)
pfg@premieradvisor.com

Wayne started in the financial services business after he completed a certified financial planning program in 1983. He previously had been involved in income tax preparation and business planning for a select group of clients. As he added a financial-planning approach to his consulting work, he realized that his clients were having difficulty implementing recommendations with a major brokerage firm or an insurance agent. Trying to implement the plan in an environment dominated by sales- and transaction-oriented practices was disastrous to the long-term strategies needed for a plan to be successful. Fee-based services were almost nonexistent for the moderately wealthy.

Wayne initially became a stockbroker at a major firm and stayed there through the beginning of the financial-planning era. His experience included a review of most of the complex and often poorly conceived investment strategies that came out of Wall Street. In 1989 he had the opportunity to take the firm private; thus the beginning of Premier Financial Group as an SEC RIA (Registered Investment Advisor). He gained an understanding of the overwhelming benefits of indexing and asset class investing. That began his personal and professional commitment to creating successful, long-term client relationships incorporating fee-only wealth management and high-touch, personalized client service.

Wayne believes the most important element of wealth management is investment portfolio management. To maintain the highest standards of portfolio management, he uses an institutional index and asset allocation investment program. He has also incorporated a sophisticated estate-planning and tax-efficient investment management program to help his clients retain the maximum amount of their wealth.

He also enjoys educating his clients on the common pitfalls and hazards of the financial industry: "It's imperative that we help our clients reduce and manage their decisions by creating financial portfolios based on sound investment strategies rather than media hype."

Most Satisfying Success Story

A family Wayne worked with achieved a level of financial success far beyond what most people ever attain. They first came to Wayne with a still active corporate retirement plan from a small business they had owned. Over time and working closely with their accountant, complex issues were solved and the assets were distributed to the family's individual retirement accounts.

All this activity naturally evolved into the need for comprehensive estate planning. Wayne worked closely with the clients' attorney to establish a sophisticated living trust as well as adding liquidity to the private investment wealth of the family. As trust and confidence grew, they incorporated a wealth replacement trust and ultimately transferred substantial insurance funds to their estate tax-free and to the heirs to help reduce the burden of estate taxes. There was a sense of financial peace of mind that allowed them to turn their attention to long-term charitable contributions. This resulted in converting some highly taxed assets into a donor-advised charitable fund with a community foundation. All this was accomplished successfully before the death of the husband.

Douglas W. Baker, CFP, CFS, President
Meridian Capital Management, Inc.
4332 Cerritos Avenue, Suite 100
Los Alamitos, CA 90720
(714) 229-2266
Dbaker@AFGWEB.com

Douglas started in the financial services business out of high school, working in the accounting realm. Twelve years later, in 1980, he started a financial-planning practice and returned to school for the CFP designation. As an accountant he had prepared books and records for companies or completed tax returns, both of which were nothing more than a matter of recording the past. Re-creating financial activity didn't seem as exciting as working with people to plan for the future.

His specialty is the design and management of a portfolio and making a client feel comfortable with money.

Most Satisfying Success Story

Douglas had a client who was a police officer four years from retirement. He was very nervous about the prospect of making his retirement pay last for the rest of his life, and so Douglas developed a series of strategies that included taking no more vacations (to accrue pay), increasing deferred compensation, and working overtime at least two days a month.

The officer followed every piece of advice to the letter and then retired and moved out of state. For years Douglas heard nothing from him, until one day he called to take Douglas to lunch. During that meal the man thanked Douglas for giving him a "better life" and a better retirement than he had ever dreamed was possible.

Unfortunately, the man died last year, 15 years after retiring. His daughter called to tell Douglas how her father had lived so well during his retirement. Douglas feels it's rather humbling to think his advice had so much of an impact on someone's life.

Leonard A. Reinhart, Founder and Chairman
Lockwood Financial Group Suite 310
10 Valley Stream Parkway
Malvern, PA 19355
(610) 695-9150

Leonard is recognized as one of the founders of the wrap fee industry. He started his career in 1978 at E.F. Hutton and was directly responsible for developing programs that introduced institutional-level professional investment management services to the individual investor marketplace. Under his leadership, the organization dominated its market, ultimately gathering more than $70 billion in assets under management and serving over 200,000 clients.

Leonard founded the Lockwood family of companies in 1995. Lockwood Financial Services, Inc., the broker/dealer, is the first investment advisory firm specifically designed to provide a turn-key investment consulting platform to independent broker/consultants, investment advisors, and financial planners. Through Lockwood, advisors can access the asset management services of a large universe of highly regarded institutional money managers, choosing among more than 120 investment-style alternatives to create customized investment programs for their clients.

In 1998 Leonard was named one of the "Power Fifty—the Most Influential People in Financial Services" by *Ticker,* a leading industry publication. He serves on the board of governors of the Money Management Institute and on the board of directors of the Institute of Investment Management Consultants. He is frequently quoted on the industry by *The Wall Street Journal, Forbes,* and other major financial publications and is a regular contributor to *Registered Representative* magazine, a leading industry publication. He has appeared on financial programs broadcast over the CNN and CNBC networks.

Jeff Saccacio
PricewaterhouseCoopers L.L.P.
(213) 356-6058
jeff.saccacio@us.coopers.com

Jeff is partner in charge of the West Coast Personal Financial Services Practice for PricewaterhouseCoopers L.L.P. He specializes in planning for high-net-worth individuals, entrepreneurs, and closely held businesses and has extensive estate- and trust-planning experience.

Jeff is a certified public accountant and holds a bachelor of business administration degree from the University of Notre Dame. He also holds a chartered financial consultant (ChFC) designation from the American College. He has earned a personal financial specialist (PFS) designation from the American Institute of Certified Public Accountants.

Don Schreiber, Jr., CFP, President and CEO
Wealth Builders, Inc.
34 Sycamore Avenue, Suite 1-E
Little Silver, NJ 07739
(800) 772-5810 or (732) 842-4920
(732) 842-8049 (Fax)

Don is the founder, president, and CEO of Wealth Builders, Inc., in Little Silver, New Jersey. He is a certified financial planner and member of the FPA (Financial Planning Association), ICFP, the IAFP, and the IAFP's Broker/Dealer Division. He currently holds the following NASD licenses: Series 27, 24, 28, 7, 63, and 65. In 1984 Don founded Wealth Builders, Inc., a financial-planning and advisory firm. In 1988 he founded Wealth Builders Equity Corporation, an independent NASD broker dealer which was sold in 1996 to Investors Financial Group (IFG). In 1992 Don founded Wealth Builders Capital Management, an institutional-quality, fee-based money management business.

Before forming the Wealth Builders Group of companies, Don was extensively involved in managing a family-owned manufacturing business. In addition, he has spent nearly two decades providing small and medium-size business owners with strategic plan development, management consultation, and financial advisory services.

He has developed a proprietary strategic business plan development process that helps a successful financial professional transform his or her sales practice into an institutionalized business with exceptional growth potential and enhanced value. Because of his extensive experience, Don is often called on by the press to provide his perspective on issues ranging from strategic business and financial planning to investment market analysis. Don earned a bachelor of science in business and finance from Susquehanna University in 1977.

John A. Meier
10955 Lowell Street, Suite 420
Overland Park, KS 66210
(913) 451-1636
tierneyj@faskc.com

John is general counsel for Financial Advisory Service, Inc., a financial-planning firm. He oversees administrative and regulatory issues.

Mark Sumsion, CEO
Strategic Capital Management, Inc.
2230 North University Parkway, 9-C
Provo, UT 84604
(800) 279-3377
mark@scmi.com

Mark started in the financial services business in 1989, when he founded Strategic Capital Management with Dennis Slothower and Duane Wyckoff.

They were brokers for Shearson Lehman Hutton in the 1980s and developed a trading system for financial futures. By the mid-1980s they began to apply those risk-adjusting strategies to mutual fund money management. Those strategies enabled them to protect their clients from the substantial declines in the stock market in 1987. They were ahead of the times when they wanted to apply their risk-adjusting strategies in a wrap fee account for no-load mutual funds management. In the 1980s major wire houses were oriented to the selling of load mutual funds and didn't adopt wrap fee management until the 1990s. This put them in direct conflict between doing what was best for their clients and doing what was best for the firm, which ultimately caused them to be fired from Shearson. But it was a case of "don't throw me into the briar patch," as it enabled them to establish their firm.

Mark's specialty is mutual fund selection (including variable annuity subaccounts), allocation, and timing.

A P P E N D I X

B

VARIABLE LIFE INSURANCE

I T IS IMPORTANT TO NOTE THAT ALL INVESTMENT PRODUCTS have different tax ramifications while one is living and after one's death, and this may play a role in when and how these vehicles are used.

Life insurance is one of the more complex products. Let's very briefly discuss the different types of life insurance and the benefits and negatives of each one.

One major classification of life insurance is *term,* which means simply the amount of time. The term can be 1 year or 5, 10, 15, 20, or 30 years, until age 65. The insurance company makes a promise that if the client dies within that term, the insurance company will pay the client's beneficiary the death benefit.

The company will give a client a very low rate for a period, but after that period, the client must requalify. If he or she does not, term rates could grow as much as three or four times. If the insurance is needed for a longer period, term may not be the right type of insurance.

The other broad category of life insurance is *permanent,* or *whole life.* This type of insurance has two factors attached to it: the mortality charges, which is the death benefit side, and an accrual side where any excess or any mortality charges go into a side account and are invested in various funds (whether long-term bonds or mutual fund–like accounts). That cash value then allows the policy cost to be reduced over a period of time, and people are able to afford this for their whole lives.

As a person gets older, the cost of dying increases, and therefore, the cost of term insurance goes up dramatically after age 50. Less than 2 percent of death benefits are paid on term insurance. For long-term benefits, universal life insurance is far better and more cost-efficient, with a decreasing form of protection and an increasing form of cash value.

A third type of insurance is called *universal life insurance.* This type is flexible. The client can increase or reduce the death benefit and also can increase or reduce the deposit based on the contract. The downside risk is that failure to pay the premiums will result in loss of the death benefit.

The fourth type of insurance is called *variable life or variable universal life* insurance. This type works like whole life insurance. It gives the client a level death benefit and guarantees the death benefit for the life of the contract; however, the client must pay the premiums.

Variable universal life insurance has become very popular since the 1986 tax laws. It can be used in risk management for protection, or it can be totally creative for maximum accumulation and tax efficiency.

Insurance also helps in business equalization such as a buy/sell partnership because cash flow is so important for companies if something should happen to one of the key players. It also reduces IRS costs. Life insurance is the cheapest substitute for taxes one can find.

Purchasing life insurance probably requires professional help as much as does any other investment, since you have to compute how much income you need, what cash flow structures you have to replace, and what your goals are. Until you have a proper risk management study done for you, you may be buying too much or too little. The rule of thumb is five or six times your earnings. That is very, very rough. Only with a competent advisor can you accurately determine how much and what kind of insurance to buy.

ANNUITY
PAYMENT OPTIONS

THE FOLLOWING SECTION WILL OUTLINE THE VARIOUS PAYMENT OPTIONS you can select once you decide to receive the income from an annuity as either fixed or variable.

Life Annuity

The entire account value is converted to a monthly income stream that is guaranteed for as long as the annuitant lives; he or she receives payments until death. This is true whether the annuitant dies in the first year or after payments have been received for more than 30 years. This settlement option is the purest form of insuring that the annuitant does not outlive his or her financial assets.

To illustrate, let's use the example of the Carters. When Mr. Carter is 65 years of age, he decides to receive payments from his variable annuity under the life annuity option. Let's say he has accumulated a value of $200,000; his monthly payments for a variable annuitization start at $1256. If his net investment returns are 4 percent and he lives only to age 70, he will receive $37,680 in benefits; the difference of $124,640 ($200,000 less $75,360) will be lost to his heirs. By contrast, if he lives to age 90, he will receive $1256 each month and collect a total of $376,800 in benefits, significantly in excess of the annuity's accumulated value of $200,000.

To illustrate the value of a variable annuitization, if he had received an 8 percent growth rate on his investments for five years, his benefit would have been $81,432, or $6072 more than the 4 percent annuitization benefit. Over the course of his lifetime, until his death at age 90, the total benefit received as income during a variable annuitization with 8 percent growth would have been $641,600, or nearly double the fixed benefit.

SUMMARY. The annuitant is guaranteed a lifetime income. At the death of the annuitant, all payments cease and the annuity is without value. No minimum number of payments is guaranteed.

ADVANTAGE. Payments are maximized for the life of the annuitant.

DISADVANTAGE. At the annuitant's death, the annuity has no value to his or her beneficiaries (estate).

Life with Period Certain

The income stream is guaranteed for a specified number of years or for as long as the annuitant lives, whichever is longer.

This is a hedge against the loss of value if the annuitant dies shortly after the contract is annuitized. Under this option, the insurance company agrees to pay the annuity benefit for the longer of either the annuitant's lifetime or a certain period of years. Most insurance companies offer a choice of the period certain, such as 10, 15, or 20 years. If the guaranteed period exceeds the life expectancy of the annuitant, then the benefit is assumed to be a period certain without life expectancy risk and the payments are reduced substantially.

In our example of Mr. Carter, age 65, if he decides to annuitize his variable annuity contract for $200,000 under a life with 5-year certain settlement option, his monthly benefit will be approximately $1243. With a life with 10-year certain option, his monthly benefit will be approximately $1205. If he elects a life with 15-year certain, his benefit will be approximately $1164. If he selects a life with 20-year certain option, the benefit will be approximately $1130. The difference represents the amount of money the insurance company keeps to guarantee the benefit if the annuitant dies prematurely. To many, a lower monthly benefit is worth the security of a 20-year guarantee.

Let's say Mr. Carter selected the life with 20-year certain settlement option at age 65 but lived only to age 80. His beneficiaries would receive the monthly payments of $1130 each month for the next five years, the remainder of the period certain. However, if he lived to age 87, the annuity payments would cease at his death and his beneficiaries would not receive any payments from the annuity contract. This particular life with period certain provides excellent options for financial-planning situations in which there are a set number of years for a particular benefit a client desires.

SUMMARY.   The annuitant receives a lifetime income, but a minimum number of payments are made whether the annuitant lives or dies. The annuitant receives two guarantees: A certain amount will be paid periodically for the lifetime of the annuitant, and if the annuitant dies before the time-certain guarantee is satisfied (usually 5 to 20 years), the annuitant's beneficiary will receive the remaining number of guaranteed payments.

ADVANTAGES.   The annuitant will receive a lifetime income. A minimum number of periodic payments will be made.

DISADVANTAGES.   The longer the guaranteed payments, the lower the periodic payment. Payments to the beneficiaries stop after the guaranteed time payment or death.

Refund Life Annuity

The entire account value is converted to a monthly income stream that is guaranteed for as long as the annuitant lives. If the annuitant dies before the principal amount is annuitized, the balance is paid to the beneficiary.

Refund life annuity is similar to the life with period certain guaranteed option. It's a hedge against the possibility of early death. Under the refund life annuity settlement option, the insurance company will pay a monthly benefit for the life of the annuitant. At the annuitant's death, if the amount that was applied to the annuitization of the contract is more than the total of installment payments received by the annuitant during his or her lifetime, the difference is paid in a lump sum to the beneficiaries.

For example, Mrs. Carter, also age 65, purchases a single-premium nonqualified annuity with $200,000 in it. Her monthly annuity payments under the refund life annuity settlement option are $990. Since Mrs. Carter is guaranteeing that her annuitized balance will be paid out regardless of her age at death, her payments will be smaller than Mr. Carter's. If she lives to age 70, she'll receive an annuity value totaling $59,400. Since she elected the life refund annuity option, Mrs. Carter's beneficiaries will receive a lump sum from the insurance company of $140,600 (the difference between $200,000 and $59,400).

However, if Mrs. Carter lives to be 85 and collects annuity payments for 20 years, she will receive a total of $237,600. As that amount exceeds her annuity value of $200,000, her beneficiaries will not receive anything upon her death.

SUMMARY.   The annuitant receives a lifetime income while protecting his or her heirs from losing the unused value of the amount annuitized. If premature death occurs, the heirs receive a lump sum.

ADVANTAGES.   The annuitant will receive a lifetime income. The principal balance is guaranteed to be paid out if death occurs prematurely.

DISADVANTAGES. The monthly income is reduced because of the higher risk to the insurance company of returning all funds not paid out during annuitization.

Joint Survivor Life Annuity

The income stream is guaranteed for as long as either annuitant lives (for example, you or your spouse).

Under the joint survivor annuity the insurance company will pay benefits during the joint lifetimes of two individuals. Often the two people are husband and wife, although there's no requirement that it be that way. They do have to be individuals, not a trust or corporation, since those entities do not have a life expectancy. Under the joint survivor life annuity option, the insurance company pays the full benefit amount until the death of one of the annuitants. If the settlement option is a full joint survivor annuity, the payment will continue in the full amount until the death of the surviving annuitant. Under a joint and one-half survivor annuitant settlement option, payments are made in full until the death of one of the annuitants but then are reduced to one-half of the full amount until the death of the survivor. Some insurance companies offer a joint with two-thirds survivor annuity in which the payments to the surviving annuitant are equal to two-thirds of the original full payment amount.

Let's say the Carters have accumulated $200,000 in their variable annuity. Electing the full and joint survivor annuity settlement option will result in a benefit of $972 paid to both Mr. and Mrs. Carter until the death of one of them; again, this is a further reduction in the initial monthly benefit as a result of the longer life expectancy of two people. After the first death, the same amount of $972 will continue to be paid to the survivor until his or her death. If they elect the joint and one-half survivor settlement option, the amount paid to both of them will be approximately $979 until the first death, and then the survivor will receive one-half of the benefit, or $490 each month, until his or her death.

If they elect the joint and two-thirds survivor settlement option, the Carters will receive a benefit of $975 until the first death, at which time the survivor will receive two-thirds, or $650, in benefit payments.

SUMMARY.   Periodic payments are guaranteed for the lifetimes of two or more annuitants. Payments continue until the death of the last annuitant. A husband and wife seeking a guaranteed joint lifetime income and then a guaranteed life income for the surviving spouse typically use the joint and last survivor option. Periodic payments are made to one person until his or her death. At that point, the survivor becomes the annuitant and payments are made until the death of the survivor. The periodic payments to the surviving annuitant may be lower (three-fourths to one-half of the initial amount, depending on the survivor option).

ADVANTAGE.   The annuitants are guaranteed a lifetime income.

DISADVANTAGES.   The periodic payment amount is lower for two or more annuitants and may be reduced for the surviving annuitant or annuitants.

Fixed Annuity (Period Certain)

The entire account value is fully paid out during a specified period of time.

The fixed-period payment option is probably the easiest to explain. This option allows the annuitant to receive the accumulated value of the annuity over a set number of years. For example, if Mr. Carter was age 50, he could choose to annuitize his contract and receive the benefits over a 15-year period. He would be age 65 and eligible for Social Security, plus the benefits from any retirement plans, when his annuity payments ended. Most companies offer a fixed-period payment option for periods of any length, from 5 years to 25 years.

CAUTION.   If you choose a fixed-period annuitization from an existing contract and have accumulated earnings that have not been taxed, the receipt of those earnings may be subject to a 10 percent federal penalty. One way to avoid the penalty if you need income before age 59$^{1}/_{2}$ is to select a life contingency annuitization or choose a fixed period up to life expectancy. In most cases the IRS allows this option to bypass the 10 percent federal penalty since you are receiving income for your lifetime.

Let's consider the annuity of Mrs. Carter, which has an accumulated value of $200,000. She decides to annuitize and elects the fixed-period settlement option over a five-year period. Her monthly benefits will be $3664. She will receive this benefit payment each month for 60 months, or 5 years. At the end of this time, benefit payments will cease. No further funds will remain in the annuity contract, and no further benefits will be payable. Again, the problem is that her gain will be taxable and a 10 percent federal penalty may be added. If Mrs. Carter dies during the five-year period, benefit payments will continue to be paid to her beneficiaries until the end of the fifth year.

SUMMARY.   This is a safe income option to choose for assuring the payout of the principal value. The benefit of guaranteed income for life is lost, as are tax benefits such as the ability to start before age 59$^{1}/_{2}$.

ADVANTAGE.   The income can be substantially higher since the typical payout is for less than life expectancy.

Fixed-Amount Annuities

Under the fixed-amount option, the annuitant receives benefit payments for a set amount until the annuity accumulation value, plus interest, runs out. Returning to our example, Mr. Carter has an accumulated value of $200,000. Under this payment option he could elect to receive a monthly benefit of $3000 or any amount he would prefer. The insurance company will send him a check each month for as long as the accumulated value and interest support the benefit. After the funds in the annuity are exhausted, Mr. Carter will not receive any further benefits from the contract. In the event of his death, any funds remaining in the annuity most likely will be paid to the beneficiaries. This is more commonly referred to as a systematic withdrawal. In addition to a fixed-amount option, it is possible to choose a fixed-percentage option. For instance, you could say that you want 10 percent of the current balance every year. If the balance declines, so will your income; if the balance increases, so will your income.

ADVANTAGE.   You do not give up access to your principal. Since you have not annuitized, you can access your account for additional distributions for unexpected events.

DISADVANTAGES.   Unlike life contingency options, the payments are not tax-favored. With life contingency options or period certain, you receive principal with interest, which increases your net income. With a systematic withdrawal, you receive interest first and may be subject to a 10 percent federal penalty. In addition, some annuities may penalize you for taking distributions in excess of 10 percent of the account balance during the early years.

Interest-Only Option
The interest-only option is just what it says. If Mr. Carter had $200,000 and in 1998 received a net rate of return of 10 percent, he would receive $20,000 that year, which would be fully taxable; if it is received before age 59½, the full amount may be subject to a 10 percent federal penalty. Those who do not want to withdraw income against principal most commonly choose this option.

ADVANTAGE.   You have access to your income for rainy days.

DISADVANTAGES.   The income is fully taxable and can vary significantly. In down years, the income can be zero.

Lump-Sum Payment
The annuitant has the option of receiving the entire value of an annuity in a lump sum. This allows the annuitant to accumulate his or her funds in a tax-deferred manner and, if older than age 59½, withdraw the funds without a federal penalty. These assets can then be used for projects or to start a business.

ADVANTAGES.   The annuitant retains complete control of the annuity value. The total account balance can be liquidated.

DISADVANTAGES.   The annuitant is not guaranteed a lifetime income. There may be tax and penalty consequences.

INDEX

A-shares, 58
Account managers (*see* Expert advisors, Separate
    account managers)
Accumulation units, 125
ADV, 73, 148
Advisors, 68, 69
    (*See also* Expert advisors)
Alternative minimum tax, 97
Annuities, 122–133
    checklist of factors to consider, 132
    deferred, 115, 127
    fixed, 123
    flexible-premium, 128
    immediate, 127
    parties, 130, 131
    payout options, 129, 130, 204–211 (*See also*
    Annuity payment options)
    phases, 128
    rating services, 131
    single-premium, 127, 128

Annuities (*Cont.*)
    surrender charges, 126
    Swiss, 153
    variable charges, 114, 115, 124–128, 132,
        133
Annuity payment options, 129, 130, 204–211
    fixed annuity (period certain), 209, 210
    fixed-amount annuities, 210, 211
    interest only option, 211
    joint survivor life annuity, 208, 209
    life annuity, 204, 205
    life with period certain, 205, 206
    lump-sum payment, 211
    refund life annuity, 207
Asset Allocation (Gibson), 42
Asset class funds, 54
Asset protection, 147–153

B-shares, 58
Bailout provision, 123

213

Baker, Douglas W., 7, 9, 16, 50, 56, 62, 108, 115, 196

Balance growth managers, 76, 77

Banks, 69, 70

Beardstown ladies, 44

Beebower, Gilbert, 34

Bergen, Marilyn R., 5, 8, 14, 19, 22, 36, 61, 107, 113, 118, 120, 132, 139, 190

Big five, 12–16

Black box investment strategy, 21

Blank management, 71

Bowen, John J., Jr., 5, 10, 11, 13, 35, 41, 50, 55, 63, 107, 111, 139, 158, 167, 178, 187

Brinson, Gary, 34

Brokerage houses, 70, 71

C-shares, 58

Caldwell, Wayne O., 6, 8, 11, 15, 19, 21, 23, 37–40, 48, 55, 56, 108, 113, 115, 157–159, 168, 179–181, 195

Call risk, 136

Campisi, Joe, 16, 61, 139, 192

Cash management managers, 78

Cashless exercise, 101

Chambers, Larry, 79, 81, 82

Charitable planning, 159, 167–169

Charitable remainder trust (CRT), 156, 163–169

Chicago Match, 89

Closed-end funds, 142

Commitment, 3

Common Sense Investment Guide-How We Beat the Stock Market and How You Can Too, 44

Company stock options (*see* Stock options)

Computerized matching system, 90

Contact information (names/addresses), 185–200

Contingency fees, 148

Convertible bonds, 77

CRT, 156, 163–169

Dartboard approach to stock selection, 54, 55

Day trading, 80, 83

Deer in the headlights syndrome, 6

Deferred annuities, 115, 127

"Determinants of Portfolio Performance" (Brinson/Hood/Beebower), 34

Detrended stochastics, 55

Diamonds, 141

Digital stock market (DSM), 89

Diversification, 34–37

Dollar cost averaging, 37

DSM, 89

Due diligence process, 72–74

Durable power of attorney, 176

E-trading, 79–92

  cautionary notes (warnings), 91, 92

  delays, 82, 91

  fast markets/volatility, 91, 92

  future trends, 89–91

  levels of quotes, 84, 85

  middlemen, 88, 89

  Nasdaq, 87, 88

  NYSE, 86, 87

  types of investors, 83

  types of orders, 85, 86

Earnings growth approach, 76

Electronic matching systems, 90

Emerging growth managers, 76

Emotional risk, 26, 27

End objective, 4

Escape clause, 123

Estate planning, 170–182

  downside/risks, 180

  experts' advice, 177–180

  GSTT, 173, 176

  precautionary measures (incompetence), 176, 177

  successful plans (example), 180, 181

  title ownership, 174

  tools, 182

  trusts, 175

  will, 172, 175, 176

ETFs, 141–143

Evensky, Harold, 5, 20, 35, 47, 112, 120, 138, 158, 168, 187

Exchange-traded funds (ETFs), 141–143

Exempt assets, 150, 151

Exercise date, 100

Exercise price, 100

Expert advisors, 185–200

Expiration date, 100

Expiration period, 98

Fast markets, 92

Federal Reserve, 54

Ferrara, V. Raymond, 6, 7, 14, 17, 22, 47, 50, 62, 106, 112, 139, 156, 167, 179–182, 188
Financial experts (names/addresses), 185–200
Financial planning, 7–10
Financial Success in the Year 2000 and Beyond (Nohr), 165
Five important things to know, 12–16
Fixed-amount annuities, 210, 211
Fixed annuity, 123
Fixed annuity (period certain), 209, 210
Fixed-income managers, 78
Flexible-premium annuity, 128
Floor broker, 87
Foss-Erickson, Kim, 9, 12, 36, 108, 139, 192
French, Ken, 49

Generation-skipping transfer tax (GSTT), 173, 176
Gibson, Roger, 42
GRANT, 175
Grant date, 100
GRAT, 181
GRIT, 175
Growth managers, 75, 76
GRUNT, 175
GSTT, 173, 176
Guaranteed Income for Life (Lane), 122
Gurus, 21, 44

Hargrave, Stan, 63, 139, 193
Health care directive, 177
Homestead, 151, 153
Honoring the two-sided market, 87, 88
Hood, Randolph, 34
Hopewell, Lynn, 4, 8, 10, 13, 17, 20, 22, 47, 50, 54, 111,
121, 155, 178, 180, 182, 185

i-shares, 141
ICO, 95, 96
Immediate annuity, 127
Incentive stock options (ISO), 95, 96
Income growth managers, 77
Independent investment management firms, 71
Individually managed account, 65–68
Industry rotators, 78
Insurance, 149, 201–203
Interest rate risk, 136

Internet trading (*see* E-trading)
Investment noise, 41–45
Investment pornography, 42
Investor risk, 26, 27
Irrevocable trusts, 175

Joint survivor life annuity, 208, 209
Joint tenancy with right of ownership, 174

Kautt, Glenn G., 10, 13, 20, 35, 47, 48, 50, 56, 61, 111, 120, 156, 158, 177, 178, 180, 182, 186

Large cap growth managers, 76
Level I screen, 84
Level II screen, 84
Level III screen, 85
Levels of quotes, 84, 85
Life annuity, 204, 205
Life insurance, 201–203
Life with period certain, 205, 206
Limit order, 85, 91
Limited liability company (LLC), 148
Loss principal, 29

M&E charges, 126
Manager styles, 74–78
Market impact costs, 89
Market makers, 88
Market order, 85, 91
Market specialist, 87
Market timing, 34, 53–56
Meier, John A., 147, 200
Money managers (*see* Expert advisors, Separate account managers)
Monte Carlo simulation, 16
Moran, Patrick, 16, 61, 108, 193
Muldowney, Thomas, 7, 36, 62, 107, 189
Municipal bond funds, 114, 134–140
Mutual funds, 57–63
    closed-end funds, 142
    growth of, 65
    individually managed accounts, compared, 65, 66
    municipal bonds, 134–140
    NAV, 58
    open-ended vehicles, as, 142
    risk, 106

Mutual funds (*Cont.*)
  sales charges, 58
  selection of, 60–63
  taxes, 106
  transaction costs, 59
Names and addresses (expert advisors), 185–200
Nasdaq, 87, 88
NAV, 58
Net asset value (NAV), 58
New York Stock Exchange, 86, 87
No-load mutual funds, 58
Nohr, Tom J., 4, 22, 108, 116, 165, 194
Noise investors, 41–45
Nonqualified stock option (NQSO), 96, 97
Norex exchange, 90
NQSO, 96, 97
Obstacles, 20–22
Offshore asset protection trusts, 151, 152
On-line investing (*see* E-trading)
Online Broker and Trading Directory, The
  (Chambers), 81
Optimization, 39
Over-the-counter (OTC) market, 87

Pelky, Lance A., 22, 49, 139, 193
Perfect investment, 28
Performance expectations, 46–50
Permanent insurance, 202
Perot, Ross, 135
Personal umbrella insurance, 149, 150
Planning process, 16–20
Postseparation expiration date, 100
Power of attorney, 149, 176, 177
Price impact costs, 89
Protection and preservation (*see* Wealth protec-
  tion and preservation)

Qualified personal residence trust (QPRT), 175,
  176
Qualified plans, 117–121
Quality growth managers, 76

Rating services:
  annuities, 131
  bonds, 138
Reality of investing, 28
Refund life annuity, 207

Reinhart, Leonard A., 64, 197
Relative value managers, 75
Rembert, Donald, 185
Riding the yield curve, 111
Risk, 25–32
  bonds, 136
  investor, 26, 27
  mutual funds, 106
Risk tolerance, 29–31

S&P 500, 109
Saccacio, Jeff J., 94, 198
Schreiber, Don, Jr., 25, 199
Schubert, Kelley, 6, 15, 18, 21, 24, 48, 55, 62,
  107, 112, 138, 167, 179, 182, 191
SEC 13F filings, 73
Security selection, 34, 54, 55
Separate account managers, 64–78
  advisors, 68, 69
  due diligence process, 72–74
  individually managed account, 65–68
  manager styles, 74–78
  selecting a money manager, 68–70
  types of money managers, 69–72
Shilanski, Floyd L., 6, 50, 194
Single-premium annuity, 127, 128
Size of companies, 38
Slothower, Dennis, 200
Small cap growth managers, 76
SOES, 89
Specialists, 87, 88
Spiders, 141, 142
Spread:
  annuities, 123
  stock options, 96
Springing power of attorney, 176
Step-up in basis, 115, 173
Stock market orders, 85, 86
Stock options, 93–101
  alternative minimum tax, 97
  cashless exercise, 101
  expiration period, 98
  funding, 100, 101
  ISOs, 95, 96
  key dates, 99, 100
  NQSOs, 96, 97
  postseparation issues, 99

Stock options (*Cont.*)
   stock swapping, 101
   survivor implications, 99
   taxes, 97, 101
   vesting, 98
Stock swapping, 101
Stop limit order, 86
Stop order, 86
Success stories, 10–12, 186–197
Successful client relationship, 49, 50
Sumsion, Mark, 54, 60, 200
Sweetheart wills, 175
Swiss annuity, 153
Tax-efficient investing, 105–116
Tax engineering, 107
Taxes:
   annuities (*see* Annuities)
   death benefit, 115
   ETFs, 141–143
   GSTT, 173, 176
   municipal bond funds, 134–140
   qualified plans, 117–121
   step-up in basis, 115, 173
   stock options, 97, 101
   tax-efficient investing, 105–116
Tenancy by the entirety, 151
Term insurance, 201, 202
13F filing, 73

Time horizon, 31
Total return distribution policy, 109
2 year/1 year rule, 95

Universal life insurance, 202

Value companies, 38
Value managers, 74, 75
Variable annuity, 114, 115, 124–128, 132, 133
Variable universal life insurance, 115, 202
Vesting, 98
Vesting date, 100
Volatility, 31, 91

Wealth protection and preservation:
   asset protection, 147–153
   insurance on accounts, 149
   legal steps to protect assets, 148–153
   WRTs, 154–159
Wealth replacement trusts (WRTs), 154–159
Wealth transfer:
   charitable remainder trusts, 163–169
   estate planning, 170–182 (*See also* Estate planning)
Whole life insurance, 115, 202
Wrong, when things go, 22–24
WRTs, 154–159
Wyckoff, Duane, 200

ABOUT THE AUTHOR

Michael Lane is president of the Advisor Resources division of AEGON Financial Services Group, Inc., a major provider of insurance and investment products. A contributing editor to *Personal Financial Planning*, *Investment Advisor*, and *Financial Planning*, Lane is frequently quoted in *Barron's*, *The New York Times*, and other financial publications. His previous books include *Guaranteed Income for Life*.